GIELGUD

GIELGUD

an Actor and his time

In Collaboration With
John Miller and John Powell

Clarkson N. Potter, Inc./Publishers NEW YORK
DISTRIBUTED BY CROWN PUBLISHERS, INC.

First published in Great Britain in 1979 as *An Actor and His Time*
by Sidgwick and Jackson Limited
1 Tavistock Chambers, Bloomsbury Way
London WC1A 2SG

First American edition published in 1980 by
Clarkson N. Potter, Inc.
Distributed by Crown Publishers, Inc.
One Park Avenue, New York, New York 10016

Library of Congress Cataloging in Publication Data

Gielgud, John, Sir, 1904–
 Gielgud: An actor and his time.

 Bibliography: p.
 Includes index.
 1. Gielgud, John, Sir, 1904– 2. Actors—
Great Britain—Biography. I. Miller, John, 1937–
joint author. II. Powell, John, joint author.
III. Title.
PN2598.G45A29 1980   792'.028'0924 [B]   80-15080
ISBN: 0-517-541793

10 9 8 7 6 5 4 3 2 1

To Ralph and Mu Richardson
With gratitude and affection

John Gielgud with John Powell and John Miller during the
recording of the BBC Radio series *An Actor and his Time*

When I was first approached by John Miller and John Powell of
the BBC to record a long series of radio interviews about my life
and career in the theatre, I agreed with some reluctance. I spoke
off the cuff, not knowing beforehand the questions that John
Miller would put to me, and I found that as I talked many other
episodes and memories sprang to my mind, so that our conversations often went off at a tangent. John Powell and John Miller prepared the final tapes, compressing and editing where they thought
necessary, and I was agreeably surprised that the programmes
were very much liked by those who heard them.

The interest they aroused led to the question of publishing the
talks in book form, and this meant that a good deal of reconstruction, rewriting and editing has been necessary. This work has been
done by John Powell and John Miller, and John Goldsmith helped
me in the final reshaping and cutting. I am duly grateful to them
and to the publishers, all of whom have laboured to create a read-
able book out of the informal conversations from which it first
originated.

John Gielgud

June 1979

Contents

List of Illustrations

Where sources are not credited, photographs come from John Gielgud's archives and names of photographers are no longer available

The Gielgud-Terry Family Tree

ANIELA ASZPERGEROWA (1816–1902)

BENJAMIN TERRY = SARAH BALLARD (1818–1896) (1817–1892)

Aniela = Adam Gielgud

3 others KATE = Arthur Lewis (1844–1924)

ELLEN=(a) G. F. Watts (1847–1928) (b) CHARLES KELLY (c) JAMES CAREW

(by Edward Godwin)

Frank Gielgud = Kate Janet Lucy MABEL   EDITH CRAIG   GORDON CRAIG = May Gibson (1868–1958)

Lewis   Val   JOHN   Eleanor

GEORGE   MARION   FLORENCE = William Morris   2 others   FRED = JULIA NEILSON
         (1853–1930)   (1855–1896)   (1864–1932) (1869–1957)

                 OLIVE   3 others   PHYLLIS = (a) CECIL KING   DENNIS = MARY GLYNNE
                                                    (b) HERON CARVIC

*Names in capital letters indicate members of
the family on, or connected with, the stage*

CHAPTER
ONE

1904–1921

The house where I was born, in April 1904, was steep and chilly. It stood in the Old Brompton Road, in South Kensington, and the horse-drawn traffic, vans, cabs and carriages roared and clattered along outside, noisier even, I seem to remember, than the lorries and cars so soon to take their place. In winter the bedrooms and bathrooms were particularly cold. I hated the tepid baths and the icy, linoleum-covered floors which surrounded them; the occasional hip-bath, allowed only when I was ill, and taken in front of the nursery fire, with a big towel being warmed on the high fender, was a luxury to which I greatly looked forward.

Winter too brought the fogs, impenetrably thick. I would find my way home holding one hand in front of me for fear of colliding with someone coming in the opposite direction, while with the other I tapped along the railings with a stick.

In the main, though, my memories of a London childhood are happy ones. I remember the uniforms worn by so many different kinds of people. Maids wore caps and aprons; messenger-boys, who delivered parcels and telegrams and whose arrival, with news of accidents or deaths, was always dreaded, had pillbox caps worn on one side with a strap under the chin. Then there was the muffin-man with his big dinner-bell and the tray on his head covered with a green baize cloth, and the knife-grinder with his wheel and treadle. The coalmen had grimy faces under black shiny caps, with broad flaps at

15

As Mark Antony (second from right) in a
production at Hillside school, Godalming

the back to protect their necks and shoulders, and black corduroys buckled under the knees, like Alfred Doolittle in the second act of Shaw's *Pygmalion*. The huge coal-cart would grind to a halt at our front door and the men, jumping down to unload the sacks, would carry them on their shoulders through the gate and shovel their contents into the cellar through a round hole covered by a metal plate.

Dressing and undressing were lengthy procedures in those days and I tended to dispose of them as rapidly as possible. There were so many accessories to cope with–vests and long underpants, sock-suspenders, buttons, braces, cufflinks, collar studs, detachable collars, waistcoats and ties. Tying a bow was always a great problem, for made-up bowties were considered caddish and deplorable. Women had to wrestle with an equally formidable series of garments: drawers and petticoats, hooks and eyes, corsets, camisoles; hats, veils, muffs, handbags, card-cases and umbrellas in the daytime; teagowns or long dresses with flowing skirts, elbow-length gloves, aigrettes and fans in the evening. The fine details of costume absorbed me even before I came to observe them in the theatre with a professional eye.

Sunday was the day on which we children were expected to spend some of the time with my father. During the week he left for the City early every morning and did not return until six o'clock, when he would sometimes call on us in the nursery for half an hour and occasionally play the piano for us. He had a charming gift of playing by ear and could improvise quite ambitiously on classical themes. After Sunday lunch, when he presided over a large joint which my grandmother, Kate Terry, and an aunt or two were often invited to share, my father would set out on a long walk, usually accompanied by me and one of my brothers. For these excursions, of course, more dressing-up was required: hats, gloves, mufflers and overcoats in cold weather; boots and galoshes in wet weather; walking-sticks and straw hats in the summer months.

We walked a great deal in my boyhood. No one I knew had cars until the twenties, though I do have a vivid memory of an excursion with my grandmother in a hired electric brougham, a strange contraption without a bonnet, whose driver sat high in front and steered by means of a long curved handle. A tremendous storm broke as we were proceeding along Chiswick High Street. Enormous hailstones hit the roof of the brougham and bounced off the pavements as we sat huddled together, expecting to be electrocuted by the lightning at any moment. The machine was completely immobilized for ten minutes and the unfortunate chauffeur was soaked to the skin.

Sunday walks with my father often included visits to museums and picture galleries. Sometimes we went to concerts, either at the Queen's Hall or the Albert Hall, which was nearer home. At the Albert Hall we always had to sit on the very hard benches by the organ, because my father was convinced that they were the only seats not affected by the dreadful echo. I was apt to fidget a good deal during a long performance and would complain afterwards to my brother that I found the theatre a far more exciting place, but now I am infinitely grateful for that introduction, forced on me by my father, to the fascination of music and pictures. At the Albert Hall I heard the great Chaliapin, then at the end of his long career, a magnificent giant of a man with wavy white hair who surveyed a tiny notebook through his gold lorgnette as he checked the words of his programme. I was greatly impressed too by the pianists — Rosenthal and Rachmaninov — and by the beauty of Kreisler's violin playing, from the moment when he first lifted the instrument to his shoulder, to the awed silence of the audience as he lowered it at the end of the piece, before the applause crashed out and he smiled and bowed with infinite grace and charm. Vladimir de Pachmann was exquisite as an interpreter of Chopin, though his antics on the platform were somewhat grotesque. He would grimace and mutter to himself and sometimes to the audience. 'Chopin crying', he would exclaim during a sad nocturne, for the benefit of the people sitting in the three front rows. On one occasion he refused to begin until two men (his 'keepers', my father told me) were brought on to the platform to readjust his piano stool. They were even required to slip two pieces of writing paper under one leg of the piano which Pachmann maintained was not correctly balanced.

One Sunday morning my parents took me to Hyde Park before lunch. We passed the smart riders in Rotten Row to reach the carriage drive by Hyde Park Corner. Here, between Hanover Gate and the Achilles Statue, so-called Society was still to be seen between the hours of eleven and twelve disporting themselves in the fashionable promenade known as Church Parade.

Several distinguished ladies were pointed out to me, including Mrs Asquith, the wife of the Prime Minister. I had seen her once before at a Royal Academy Private View, hopping like a raven in a black feathered hat from one gallery to another and criticizing the exhibits in a raucous voice. I was fascinated by the sight of another lady, heavily made up, with black patches on her cheek and chin like an eighteenth-century marquise, and very fantastically over-dressed and hatted. 'Ah!' my mother whispered, 'that is Lady Alexander. She is dressed by the famous couturiers Reville and Rossiter and they say she is given her clothes by them for nothing because she is such a good advertisement.' Lady Alexander's husband, Sir George, who died in 1918, was, of course, the famous actor-manager of the St James's Theatre, and had brought to it a long series of distinguished productions. The theatre in King Street had an elegant auditorium, decorated in green and gold, but rather steep and clumsily designed: pillars unfortunately obscured the stage from a number of seats.

Lady Alexander managed to survive the disappearance of Church Parade and, long after the Great War was over, continued to exploit her dress-sense. I saw her again one night at a ball at Claridges, still wearing the black patches (but now crowned with an elaborate white wig), tightly corseted under a sheath of white satin, and foxtrotting with a succession of very personable young men. My last memory of her is curiously grotesque and somewhat tragic too. In 1945 I was directing a revival of *Lady Windermere's Fan* at the Haymarket Theatre, and was sitting in the stage box on the opening night in my usual state of trepidation when I suddenly noticed a figure in the front row of the stalls that could only be Lady Alexander, though all I could see was the back of her white coiffure, her upturned nose and the collar of a purple velvet cloak hunched about her shoulders. During the intervals she did not move, but a number of people went up to her and she seemed to talk with animation. When the play was over and the auditorium began to empty, two men suddenly appeared from nowhere. They lifted Lady Alexander from her seat, wrapping her cloak round her as if she were a doll about to be packed into a box for Christmas, and carried her bodily past the rows of empty seats. Then, pushing open the door which led from the stalls to the box where I was still sitting, they rushed past me with their burden up the steps leading to the ante-room. From here there is a long passage leading to the Royal Entrance in Suffolk Street, where her car was obviously waiting. The incident was over in a flash but it was a strange farewell appearance for such a sensational personality, and it haunted me for days after.

My mother was the daughter of Kate Terry-Lewis, the eldest of her four daughters, only one of whom, my aunt Mabel, went on the stage. In 1893, when she was twenty-seven, my mother married Frank Gielgud, who was a stockbroker. She had four children, Lewis, Val, myself and my sister Eleanor, who was three years younger than me.[1]

Grandmother Kate—she of the electric brougham—was the eldest child of Ben and Sarah Terry, both actors, and her next sister was the great actress Ellen Terry, Irving's leading lady for a quarter of a century. Another sister was Marion Terry, a beautiful actress, and her brother Fred, the youngest of that generation, also had a distinguished career on the stage.

Grandmother was herself a successful actress.[1] As a child she worked with the Charles Keans, then with Fechter in London and Manchester. She played about 100 parts before she retired in 1867, at the age of twenty-three, to marry my grandfather, Arthur Lewis, who was a very fashionable haberdasher with a shop called Lewis & Allenby's in Conduit Street. He had a beautiful house, Moray Lodge, on Campden Hill, was an amateur painter and singer and a friend of Dickens and Mark Lemon. Grandmother Kate reigned on Campden Hill as Mrs Arthur Lewis and entertained in a very big way, with concerts and enormous parties. There was a conservatory, terraced garden, a billiard room and so on. And then Arthur Lewis lost all his money. After his death, my grandmother lived very simply and rather resentfully in an ugly little house in West Cromwell Road, and she had no grand clothes and did not give parties any more. She played bridge and had paying guests. This was a sad end to her career but she never grumbled or groused. She must have hated being out of the picture, even though many people still recognized her and paid court to her.

Recently I was returning from a trip to America, and on the way from Heathrow to Central London in the car I passed the end of the street where my grandmother had lived. Her old house was being systematically demolished by bulldozers, and as the brick walls crashed down, I could suddenly remember the look of every single room in the house, my aunt giving me biscuits from a box on a high shelf in her bedroom, and my grandmother sitting up in

Adam Gielgud, my paternal grandfather

My grandmother, Kate Terry, as Andromeda — photographed by Lewis Carroll in 1865. Kate was the first of the Terrys to make her name on the English stage

Aniela Aszpergerowa, my great-grandmother on my
father's side, with her two daughters in the 1850s

My mother, Kate Terry Gielgud,
from a portrait by John Collier

bed in a flannel nightgown with a white pigtail down her back.

My grandfather died at the turn of the century, before I was born, but I knew my grandmother well; she did not die until 1924. She saw me in quite a number of plays, and now, of course, I wish I had asked her more about her stage career, but she was then an old lady and I did not connect her with the theatre in the way that I connected Ellen and Marion and Fred, who were still acting when I was a child. But she took me to the theatre a great deal when I was a boy, usually to matinées, where she demanded – and received – a certain amount of respect from the management. They used to give her the Royal Box and we would sit there together. Tea was sent and we would sometimes go round afterwards and see the actors.

My grandparents on my father's side were both Polish but spoke perfect English, and my great-grandmother, Aniela Aszpergerowa, had been a successful actress in Lithuania, famous for her Shake-spearean roles. Her husband Wojciech was also a famous leading actor. Their daughter married Adam Gielgud, my grandfather, who had been born at sea during his parents' flight from the Polish revolution of 1830, when the Counts Gielgud lost their family seat – a castle, Zamek Gielguda, on the River Memel. Adam came to England with his wife in the 1850s or 1860s and lived there until finally retiring to Switzerland where they both died. He was a war correspondent. He had a little beard, I remember, and was very charming. My grandmother, who spoilt me rather when she was in England, was a devout Catholic. She wore a black velvet bag with a silver clasp which hung on a chain from her waist. I once went to stay with them in Vevey, where they lived in a *pension*, and my grandmother took me to see Francesca Bertini in a silent film. Often we would go to a wonderful cake shop in Montreux where they had delicious ices and coffee with cream on top. I was very greedy then, as I still am.

I was very fond of my Gielgud grandparents and they were very sweet to me, but I do not think they ever talked to me about the theatre; I did not feel that they had much to do with it – any more than my father's brother who shot big game in Africa, or his sister who was married to a very well-known academic painter in Krakow and who had nine children. Her eldest son was killed in the First War fighting against the British, while my brother was in the British Army fighting on the other side.

I had never thought that my father's side of the family was a very important influence on my acting, though Marguerite Steen, in her book about the Terry family, suggests that my Slav side was of great value to me, helping to make me more original as a performer. It is certainly true that my father had more sense of humour than my mother. He had something of the Slav temperament and was inclined to be moody. He could be very enchanting but also rather forbidding, and had a far less easy temperament than my mother. He may have given me a certain edge. If I had been a pure Terry, with the emotional facility of that family, my acting talent might have developed in a more conventional way. I have always had a tremendous feeling for Russian literature, ballet and music. I was highly amused by a comment Bernard Shaw made once in a letter to Edith Evans, when we were playing together in *The Seagull* and Shaw refused to admit that I was any good at all. Indeed, he thought my performance was so dreadful that the play was ruined every time I came on the stage. I suppose he had no idea that I had a Lithuanian background on my father's side which might have given me an insight into Russian plays and literature. 'Of course,' he wrote, 'John Gielgud, although he can be very good when he is rightly cast, couldn't possibly play anything by Chekhov, being a Terry.'

Among the Terrys Ellen was, of course, the 'Great Star'.[2] She led a somewhat irregular private life. She did occasionally come to our house, but my mother thought her restless and fidgety, and preferred the acting of her sister Marion. I fell madly in love with Ellen the first time I ever saw her on the stage. I decided that the restlessness was part of her glory, because what I remember most about her is her movement, although she was then in her seventies, deaf, rather blind and very vague. But when she came on you really believed that she was walking on the flagstones of Venice or in the fields of Windsor. She moved with an extraordinary spontaneity and grace, holding her skirts gathered in two hands or bunched up over one arm, and crossed the stage with an unforgettable impression of swiftness. In her great days it was always said that the lines in *Much Ado* – 'For look where Beatrice like a lapwing runs/Close by the ground to hear our conference' – were exactly applicable to her. Shaw said that she had a genius for standing still, when she was not making the most beautiful movements. Irving insisted on this, because he was very slow and she was very swift. She was a Pre-Raphaelite actress. She had sat for painters like Rossetti, and she had known and talked with all the great men of her time – Tennyson, Browning, Ruskin,

Wilde—and had learned a great deal from them. Yet she had a real humility. When you met her, you felt that she was ready to learn from children, or from anybody else with whom she came into contact. She also had a wonderful sense of humour which the rest of my aunts and uncles certainly did not.

My grandmother had a kind of heavy humour, but I always felt that she was slightly jealous of Ellen's enormous fame. She had been so very successful herself when she was young, but had given it all up to marry and have children and become a respectable Victorian matron. Ellen had three marriages, several love affairs and two illegitimate children and, although she and Irving were honoured guests in my grandparents' house, there was never that intense devotion between the sisters that biographers would like to suggest, though I was told that when my grandmother died Ellen went down and sat in her room for two or three hours, quite alone with her.

Ellen's humour, frankness and generosity were all slightly suspect to Marion, Fred and Kate who, though they were all fine actors, took the theatre dreadfully seriously. This made them extremely good in rubbish. They performed in very fustian plays. They all absorbed Irving's[3] love of romantic melodramas in which they acted with great skill and conviction. Marion was a great comedienne, marvellous in farce because she herself had no humour at all. Even though the whole family was so talented, they must have considered Ellen rather a scrapegrace. Indeed, it was a wonder that she managed to be received in all the great houses of England and America when her two children, Edith and Gordon Craig, had no official father.[4]

I was fortunate in seeing Ellen four or five times on the stage. I was only dimly aware of how difficult it was for her to go on acting: at that time she found it almost impossible to remember her lines and she could hardly see. It was said that she had strained her eyes when she was living with Edward Godwin, the father of her two children. Godwin was an architect, a thoroughly unreliable man who often failed to come home at nights, and Ellen would sit up working on his plans and drawings by candlelight.

All the Terrys had very bad memories. Marion, at the end of her life, used to go to play the big scene from *Lady Windermere's Fan*, with my aunt Mabel Terry-Lewis, her niece, at charity matinées, and I remember my mother trying to hear her go through her words at our house. She kept making endless mistakes, although she had known the part for many years.[5] However, they all had a lot of skilful ways of covering their lapses of memory, as many old actors do. Irene Vanbrugh, in her last performances, had the same trouble, but she would shout or stamp her foot or look at the other actor, making it seem as if he was the one who had dried up. This was a much more common occurrence in my days as a youthful playgoer. The prompter was often a good deal in evidence, particularly on first nights, and the audience did not mind, they thought it was all part of the fun. When I saw Ellen Terry as the Nurse in Doris Keane's *Romeo and Juliet* in 1919 she could hardly remember a word, and Basil Sydney and Leon Quartermaine, who were playing Romeo and Mercutio respectively, whispered every line in her ear, and then she said the line herself and it sounded as if she had just thought of it. One would have thought it would have made her nervous, but she still had confidence in her charisma and in the audience, and managed to enchant them just the same.

I have heard very little about her performance as Hermione in *The Winter's Tale*, one of the last big parts she played in 1906, just before her jubilee. (Tree did not play in it, though it was produced in his theatre—a man called Charles Warner played Leontes). There are some beautiful photographs of Ellen as the statue, but there is no record that I have been able to find which really discusses her performance, and I would imagine that by that time she was probably too old to create a completely new success. Perhaps when she chose the play for her jubilee year she remembered that she had made her very first appearance on the stage all those years before as the boy Mamillius in the same play, with Mrs Charles Kean as Hermione wearing a Greek wreath round her head and a crinoline with many layers of petticoats. But Ellen Terry went on playing Portia and Queen Katharine in *Henry VIII* almost until the end of her life in charity matinées and at Stratford. She probably had to go on appearing a little too long, but once she stopped acting for good she was sad and began to fail. I once visited her at her lovely farm in the country, but I felt that she was restless there, and could only really be happy when she was working in the theatre.

I saw her once on the Palace Pier at Brighton, playing the Trial scene from *The Merchant of Venice*. She had to be wheeled down that long pier in a bath chair to reach the theatre; but when she came striding on in the Trial scene you would never have thought she was a semi-invalid and an old lady, except that she had white hair under

Left: My great-aunt Ellen Terry as Beatrice in *Much Ado About Nothing*. 'It was always said that the lines:
For look where Beatrice like a
  lapwing runs
Close by the ground to hear our
  conference
were exactly applicable to her'

Right: Sir Henry Irving with Ellen Terry in *Olivia*, adapted from Goldsmith's *The Vicar of Wakefield*, at the Lyceum Theatre, 1885. 'He was very slow and she was very swift'

Below: Ellen Terry in old age

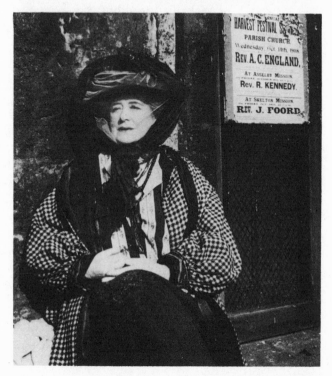

her scarlet cap. She achieved the most perfect phrasing when speaking Shakespeare, a kind of frankness which made it seem as if she had just been taught the passage in the next room by Shakespeare himself. I heard her do the 'Mercy' speech many times at charity matinées, and she never failed to thrill her audience, although she often hesitated from forgetfulness.

One of her great gifts was that she could, as Shakespeare does, suddenly drop from a very high style of speech, manner and behaviour, into something so homely and human that the whole audience was immediately touched by it. Shakespeare often demands this method: 'Dost thou not see my baby at my breast, That sucks the nurse asleep?', 'All the perfumes of Arabia will not sweeten this little hand', and 'Pray you, undo this button'. Those very simple words, when they are suddenly contrasted with the linguistic grandeur around them, can have the most superb effect on the stage. Ellen Terry knew exactly how to change gear in order to achieve the right result.

When I was a boy, I heard her read Beatrice in *Much Ado* at a private house in Grosvenor Square. Ellen came on in evening dress and a cloak, sat with a lot of amateurs on little gold chairs, and started reading very solemnly. After a scene or two she dropped the book in her lap and started to act, and it was wonderful to see this old lady suddenly turn into a young woman of twenty-five. The other actors were thrilled too, but they were also rather put out when, in the church scene, she rushed over to embrace poor Hero, a timid young girl, and a gold chair fell over, and the evening became something of a shambles.

The Terrys all had mellifluous voices which could break very easily, and a great gift for tears — a gift I seem to have inherited. Edward Gordon Craig, Ellen's son, always maintained that Ellen could not resist making an audience cry; and there was some truth in it. At the same time, she was perfectly aware of the humbug. In a scene of pathos, when she was weeping real tears for the benefit of the audience, she would turn round and whisper jokes with the actors behind her hand. She was terribly mischievous; even towards the end of her career, in 1902 when she was playing in *The Merry Wives*, she put a pin in the padding Herbert Tree was wearing as Falstaff. He got through just one scene before his whole stomach collapsed. Ellen was simply delighted! She was always full of childish fun — running down the stairs late for her cue, with her dresser doing up her dress at the back. She once said to me, 'Oh, I fell down in St Martin's Lane this morning and I was laughing so much the policeman couldn't pick me up.'

A landlady with whom I once stayed in digs in Edinburgh told me that she had had Ellen Terry to stay for a week. Ellen was always answering the door, talking to the coalman and being enchantingly interested in everybody. When the bill was presented on Saturday night it was only £8, but Ellen gave the landlady a cheque for £80. The landlady insisted on giving it back to her and was very angry that Ellen's lady companion, who was travelling with her and was supposed to look after her, had not taken the trouble to be there when the bill came to make sure there was no mistake.

It was perhaps Ellen's unconventional approach to life that made her such a great actress, and yet all her successes, except in Shakespeare, were in sentimental melodrama. When she tried to tackle contemporary plays—*Brassbound* and *Alice Sit-by-the-Fire* were both written for her by Shaw and Barrie—she could not remember the lines. Besides that, it seems that her personality was much too big for modern plays. Max Beerbohm said that she blew them out of the window with her bonny English warmth. As Lady Cicely in *Brassbound,* the part needed very precise phrasing and a certain discipline which cramped her style. Of course, in old-fashioned plays she had been able to rewrite her part and she often did. Her prompt-books show how she used to hack about plays like *The Dead Heart* and *Ravenswood,* as Irving and Fred Terry used to do. Many of the old actors used a script merely as a basis for improvization and would embroider parts and situations to suit their own style.

The Terry family were very loyal at supporting each other's performances. We all used to be there on their first nights. *Romeo and Juliet* was really Ellen's last professional engagement in London, in 1919, with Doris Keane playing Juliet. As we went into the theatre my grandmother arrived. Marion Terry came in from another door, and they kissed each other, of course. Then, I could not think why, they both turned and went by opposite doors into the theatre, down two different staircases. Grandmother came into the auditorium first, and the gallery, which in those days always applauded celebrities at first nights, began to clap and she smiled and waved her hand. Then Marion came in from the other side, and also got a very good round of applause. In the interval I said in a loud voice to Marion, 'Grandmother had a wonderful reception,' and Marion

Left: Kate and Ellen (Ellen is reflected in the mirror)

Right: My great-aunt Marion Terry, who created the part of Mrs Erlynne in *Lady Windermere's Fan*. 'Marion was a great comedienne, marvellous in farce because she herself hadn't any humour at all' replied, 'Yes, dear, I expect they thought it was me.' It was a very typical Terry sweetness. I do not think they were maliciously jealous, but there must have been, of course, a certain competition. Marion sometimes had to succeed Ellen in a play. She was supposed to be very good in Shakespeare, although I think she never played it in London. My father saw her once in Stratford as Rosalind and admired her acting very much, more than he admired Ellen's in fact. I do not know whether my parents were slightly disapproving of the Bohemian life that Ellen led, or whether it was just the restlessness and fidgets my mother complained of, but they were less enthusiastic about her than they were about Marion and Madge Kendal.

Fred Terry, who was known as 'Golden Fred', was a great jolly man, and always very kind and helpful to me.[6] But he could be alarming too—he had a most violent temper. He was an enormous eater, gourmand, gambler, as well as a splendid actor and a great personality. He married the beautiful Julia Neilson, who was a very affected, mannered actress, but who had moments of charm. He used to make her life hell at rehearsals and his company was terrified of him. To me his productions were the last link with the Irving tradition. Fred worshipped Henry Irving. I saw his productions of *The Scarlet Pimpernel* and *Sweet Nell of Old Drury* and, later on, *Much Ado*, and they seemed to have an extraordinary sweep about them, and an immense care for detail. He used to kill his company with hard work, making them rehearse all day. A new play might take as much as a year to prepare because Fred could not learn his lines and insisted on directing himself, getting into fearful rages and losing his hat by sitting on it in the stalls. All the noises behind the scenes—royal processions approaching or the Massacre of St Bartholomew—were rehearsed and executed to perfection. Make-up, clothes, scenery and lighting—everything was meticulously harmonized.

Fred and Julia toured the provinces, in competition with Martin Harvey and his wife who were also very popular. Both Fred and Martin Harvey had been members of Irving's Company, and they followed his traditions and became great provincial stars. Fred gambled his profits away while Julia spent hers all on dresses and bric-à-brac. They lived in a big house on Primrose Hill, crammed with beautiful furniture, glass and china, ate enormous meals and became vastly fat. The last time I saw them, in *The Pimpernel*, they could no longer dance the minuet. Instead, they sat on chairs on each side of the stage while the company very nervously performed the dance under the eye of the boss, who was obviously going to give them hell the moment the curtain came down. It was rather sad and funny. But Fred, in his own way, was a great actor.

He was not very happy in modern clothes, and he had a very naive approach to the theatre. He used to come and see plays that I was in, usually standing in the back of the pit so as not to be recognized. He was fearfully shocked by *The Constant Nymph* because one of the characters was an unmarried Bohemian creature who lived with a composer in the Tyrol with a lot of illegitimate children. Fred would be violent about anything in a play that he did not think was manly and noble. The heroines were white, and the villains were black, and that was that. But he had an enchanting quality. He was funny, engaging and a real card in many ways.

Many of the Terrys appeared in the Shakespeare Tercentenary performance at Drury Lane in 1916. It was a marvellous occasion and I shall never forget it. There was an amazing programme, including the whole of *Julius Caesar*. Henry Ainley played Antony and Harley Granville-Barker had rehearsed the crowd. Du Maurier and Edmund Gwenn were the First and Second Citizens: in fact, everybody in the crowd was a well-known actor or actress. H. B. Irving was marvellous as Cassius. The programme began with some music, and after *Julius Caesar* there was also a pageant made up of tableaux from Shakespeare plays in which all the actors in London appeared, framed in scenery used in the pantomime that year. Great pillars, set on broad steps, rose through the floor of the stage at Drury Lane. The players came up with their backs to the audience from below the stage and halted on the first tier, turning round to reveal themselves—to enormous applause of course—and then moving on again to make place for another group. At the very top of the steps was a bust of Shakespeare on a pedestal, and on one side stood Ellen Terry as Comedy in white, with Geneviève Ward, a very famous old actress, as Tragedy in black on the other, both holding masks, and the company all went up in groups to lay wreaths before the statue.

Fred Terry walked on in the *Much Ado* excerpt, and Ellen and Marion appeared as Portia and Nerissa. There was a story that Geneviève Ward, who was a terrible old battle-axe, made a scene because she found she was asked to share a dressing-room. She saw the list up on the board when she came into the theatre, and did not

Ellen Terry's Jubilee at Drury Lane, 1906. The Masked Dance from *Much Ado About Nothing*, designed by Edward Gordon Craig. Ellen is standing, flanked by Marion and Kate; in all twenty-two Terrys appeared in the final Masque

Right: 'Golden' Fred Terry: 'Fred would be violent about anything in a play that he did not think was manly and noble. The heroines were white and the villains were black, and that was that'

Julia Neilson, wife of Fred Terry, as Lady Blakeney in *The Scarlet Pimpernel*

notice the other names. When she opened the door of the room she found that she had been asked to share it with Ellen Terry, who peered over her spectacles and said, 'You always were a cat, Ginny!'

It was in the interval of this performance that Frank Benson, who played Caesar, was knighted.[7] After the murder scene, King George V summoned him to the Royal Box. There was no sword, so someone rushed round the corner to Simmonds, the theatrical costumiers in King Street, Covent Garden, to borrow one. The King then knighted him, whereupon great cheers rose from the huge company behind the curtain. Sir George Alexander came out to announce to the mystified audience that Benson had been knighted, and of course the audience went mad too. It made a tremendous climax to the occasion.

The Edwardian theatre of my boyhood was dominated by the great actor-managers like George Alexander, Herbert Beerbohm Tree and Gerald du Maurier.[8] At the time I accepted their style of acting completely and I suppose I longed to be like them. I thought that was the way to act. I was inclined to prefer the panache of Fred Terry (or Robert Loraine in *Cyrano*) to the naturalistic but brilliant acting of du Maurier or Hawtrey,[9] though I also admired the latters' very different style. But I had no conception of the various methods necessary to achieve such fine results. Du Maurier often put on rubbish, just as Fred Terry did. They both catered to the public taste for plays by sentimental dramatists like J. M. Barrie. Barrie is quite out of favour now. Although his plays are beautifully constructed, there is a chocolate-box side to them which is embarrassing to the modern public, but which people adored when they were written. I saw *Dear Brutus* on its first night in 1917 and afterwards in several revivals. When I directed and acted in it myself during the Second War I kept remembering how marvellous du Maurier had been as the painter Dearth. I could not touch him in the part.

Du Maurier swept away a good deal of fustian. When he staged *Interference* in the twenties he played a long dumb-show scene in which he found a murdered man before the police arrived. It was a ten-minute episode during which he kept the house enthralled. If only he had brought such skill and expertise to Ibsen and Chekhov! But he had little appreciation of great plays. He did not read much and he did not like the theatre to be taken too seriously. He preferred to give the impression that the stage was just a way of earning a living on the side, though in actual fact he was not particularly happy

Left: Mabel Terry-Lewis, the only one of Kate Terry's four daughters to become a professional actress, in 1903

Below: Sir Frank Benson, as Caliban in *The Tempest*. 'He gave what, to a young playgoer, seemed tremendous things. The thwarted walk of Hamlet; the blood-encrusted, wholly barbaric Macbeth; the patrician in Coriolanus; the zoological, unsentimentalised Caliban' – James Agate outside the theatre. My Aunt Mabel, who worked with him once or twice, was a very accomplished actress, but she had the same slightly snobbish attitude towards the theatre. She told me once that she had been in love with Guy du Maurier, Gerald's brother, who wrote the famous play *An Englishman's Home*, and was killed in the First War. I said, 'But surely you must have been in love with Gerald?' and she replied, ' In love? With an *actor*?' She took the attitude that acting was a sort of recreation and she even once asked to be excused from playing a matinée in order to go to the Derby. Du Maurier allowed her to go.

Aunt Mabel was the youngest of my mother's three sisters.[10] She was also the prettiest and the most elegant, though somewhat sharp-tongued and opinionated. At my grandmother's house there was a full-length portrait of her by John Collier, in which she was sitting in an imposing chair, dressed in a long black velvet ballgown.

As a boy, I was particularly fascinated by her because I knew she had formerly been an actress. In 1905 she had married and given up the stage to live in the country with her husband, Ralph Batley, a captain of Territorials and, presumably, well-to-do. When I was in my early teens they invited me down to stay with them in their manor-house in Dorsetshire. There were white doves on the lawn, a dairy where I would greedily lick cream from the open bowls, and delicious meals. But I was absurdly homesick and dismayed by the quiet of the country, where I had seldom been except on family holidays. I can remember sitting in the downstairs lavatory gazing ruefully at a decorative plaque over the washstand which announced, in raised capital letters, 'East or West, Home is Best'. But I liked helping to pick mushrooms in the wet fields and bringing them back to eat for breakfast. In the evening Mabel would descend in a becoming teagown and lie on the sofa with her feet up. Reassured by her charm, I became more than ever convinced that the theatre was the career I wanted to pursue. To my great delight, my aunt decided to stage a series of performances of a one-act play by Gertrude Jennings, *The Bathroom Door*. It was at that time considered, I suppose, a little daring, since all the characters appeared in dressing-gowns, night-gowns and pyjamas. I played the juvenile and Mabel was naturally the Prima Donna. We acted in village halls for the benefit of the local Women's Institute and it was all a great success.

After the First War Mabel's husband died and she decided to

36

Gerald du Maurier: His naturalistic style of acting brought him a tremendous following

employ her boundless energies by returning to the stage. She reappeared in the early twenties in a comedy by H. M. Harwood, *A Grain of Mustard Seed*, and made an immediate success. Her style and technique were quite unimpaired by her long absence from the theatre. Her carriage and diction were always faultless and she continued to act for the next twenty years, both in London and New York, in a succession of aristocratic roles which fitted her to perfection.

As a young boy I often caught a glimpse or two of the great theatrical figures of my parents' time, Sir Squire Bancroft and Sir Johnston Forbes-Robertson.[11] I would pass them as they strolled along Piccadilly in their curly-brimmed top hats and frock coats, one with wavy white hair and a monocle dangling from a moiré ribbon, the other cadaverous, with sculptured Burne-Jones features. Bancroft had retired with a fortune many years before I was born and when Lady Bancroft died he went to live in the Albany. From there he would walk each morning to his bank, where he would demand a slip with the amount of his current balance, which he would diligently examine before proceeding to lunch at the Garrick Club.

Somewhat morbidly fascinated with mortality, he always visited the bedside of friends who were ill, bearing a large bunch of black muscat grapes. He was also a faithful attendant at funerals and memorial services (as well as fashionable theatrical first nights) and was heard to remark, on his return from a cremation service—in those days something of a novelty—'A most impressive occasion. And afterwards the relatives were kind enough to ask me to go behind.'

Perhaps the most legendary theatrical figures of that time were the international star actresses, those great creatures whose names alone could fill a theatre. I saw Eleonora Duse[12] in *Ghosts* at the New Oxford Theatre in Tottenham Court Road, long since demolished. I stood at the back of the packed theatre at a matinée. Every actor in London was there and the feeling in the audience was unforgettable, a mixture of respect and awe, a sense that we would never see this great woman again. When Duse came on, the atmosphere was already electric, and she could hardly fail to make the most wonderful impression. I did not know the play very well, but Duse looked infinitely sad and distinguished with her white hair, and wearing a plain black dress with a shawl draped over her shoulders. I remember that her acting seemed very, very simple. She had marvellous hands and all her movements were weary and poetic. Here was a legendary figure whose career had spanned fifty or sixty years

38

Eleonora Duse: 'Her acting seemed very, very simple. She had marvellous hands and all her movements were weary and poetic'

of the nineteenth-century theatre, and she succeeded, to my mind, in living up to her legend, although she was evidently old and tired.

Many years later, in 1952, at a cocktail party in Hollywood, I was introduced to Charlie Chaplin. He took me aside and began to talk to me about his boyhood in London when he used to see Tree's productions from the gallery at His Majesty's. For some reason we talked about Duse. Chaplin described an occasion on which he saw her act. He began to imitate the actor who had appeared that night with Duse. He whipped out a chair and sat astride it and began to jabber bogus Italian. In a brilliant mime, he showed how the actor was enthralling the audience with a long speech when suddenly the curtains behind began to move and a little old lady came out very quietly and glided across the stage and put her hands towards the fire. Duse. And at this point the poor actor who had seemed so remarkable a moment before was completely blotted out.

The rare appearances of Sarah Bernhardt in London were just as sensational.[13] Someone once said that the atmosphere in the theatre before the curtain went up on a play of Bernhardt's was like a cage of tigers about to be released. She had a marvellous voice with an extraordinary range. This is confirmed by her gramophone records, crude as they seem now. She and Duse both worked in so many countries where the language was not their own, and where they could not count on being understood, that they had to rely on their voice skills to convey the meaning of a scene. As I do not know any Italian I could not judge Duse's diction or phrasing. In *Ghosts*, it did seem to me that she was far too romantic, not at all the kind of hard-boiled Northern hausfrau that Mrs Alving should be, but she was magically interesting.

There is a charming story about Ellen Terry and Bernhardt. After a performance at the Lyceum, Ellen and a friend, Graham Robertson (who tells the story in his reminiscences, *Time Was*), were passing the theatre where Bernhardt was playing. Ellen had a big bag of eggs. Ellen said, 'Isn't Sally B. dead yet? Let's go in and watch the last act.' So they went and sat in the pit and, after the last curtain, went round to see Bernhardt. She was extremely upset to learn that they had been in the pit and also that they had not seen the whole play. They were just about to leave when Ellen cried, 'Oh, my eggs!' and they had to rush back to the front of the house to retrieve the eggs from the pit.

Probably the most august figure and one of the last *monstres sacrés* of the Victorian era was Dame Madge Kendal.[14] I once saw her driving down Shaftesbury Avenue, red-faced and imposing, in full evening dress. For some reason her car was lighted up inside, and there she sat, bolt upright, her hair parted in the middle and screwed back into a bun, her neck and shoulders in handsome décolletage with a sparkling necklace at the throat, and her bodice tightly corseted, with the cleft between her breasts exposed as in a portrait by Ingres—an awe-inspiring sight.

Many people, including my own father, had considered Mrs Kendal the finest actress in England, a mistress of comedy and domestic drama surpassing even Ellen Terry. She seldom ventured into the classics, however, and the photographs of her as Rosalind-Ganymede—with her husband as Orlando sporting a resplendent Victorian moustache—suggest a rather over-corseted, buskined Amazon.

On her eightieth birthday Dame Madge was asked to record a speech for broadcasting, and chose to read a speech from *As You Like It*. Arriving at the BBC she was received with respectful ceremony. The director showed her where to stand and pointing to the microphone explained politely, 'That, Dame Madge, is your Orlando.' To which the old lady replied, with a gracious smile, 'Ah, my husband was better looking than that.'

One of my earliest theatrical memories is seeing Oscar Asche in *Chu-Chin-Chow*.[15] I must have been about twelve when I went with my parents. We sat in the dress circle and I was overwhelmed by the production, which fulfilled my most cherished pictorial enthusiasms, first inspired by the drawings of Edmond Dulac, Arthur Rackham and Kay Nielsen which had illustrated my books of fairy tales. Scenery and costume were far more important even than the acting to my youthful eyes.

Asche, who was the star of *Chu-Chin-Chow*, and made a fortune out of it, was also a remarkable director. One effect I remember particularly was the opening procession of servants carrying big bowls of food, like a Veronese painting; and there were donkeys and camels and beautiful girls in yashmaks. Asche himself played the wicked king of the robbers and sported gold fingernails, while his wife, Lily

Mrs Patrick Campbell and Sarah Bernhardt in *Pelléas and Mélisande*, 1904

Right: Herbert Beerbohm-Tree as Hamlet. After the first performance W. S. Gilbert said to Tree 'My dear fellow, I never saw anything so funny in my life, and yet it was not in the least vulgar'

Brayton wore an enormous fuzzy black wig and transparent Oriental draperies.

It was wartime and the troops, home on leave from the trenches, adored *Chu-Chin-Chow*. The theatre was full of khaki and blue, and there was one scene which never failed to bring the house down. It was set in the slave-market and featured tiers of beautiful girls with very little on. This scene prompted a witticism of Tree's, 'More navel than millinery!'. I used to go to *Chu-Chin-Chow* again and again, standing for hours in the pit queue and spending all my pocket money.

I had not seen much Shakespeare and though there was not a big public for the classics in those years, I did see the Benson Company in *As You Like It* at the Coronet Theatre in Notting Hill Gate. Tree had created a great fashion for Shakespeare, from the time when he built and opened his own theatre, Her Majesty's, in 1900, until he went to America in 1915. After that, no other manager dared to compete, though Granville-Barker,[16] from 1912 to 1914, did three sensational productions of Shakespeare at the Savoy, one of which, *A Midsummer Night's Dream*, I was lucky enough to see. These productions were considered very avant-garde and appealed only to a limited, high-brow audience. The general public was not interested in Barker's simple approach after Tree's lavishly spectacular productions with real rabbits and fountains and Richard II riding a real horse through the streets of London. Tree put on a great Shakespeare festival every year, at which he used to invite various touring companies to appear in his theatre, and there would be seven or eight Shakespeare plays staged there over a couple of weeks.

At the end of the First War, James Bernard Fagan took the Court Theatre and put on a series of classics, but unfortunately he starred his wife, who was not a very good actress. Although he had Maurice Moscovitch as Shylock and Godfrey Tearle and Basil Rathbone as Othello and Iago, the venture was not financially successful. It was not until the thirties that, by a lucky chance, I was able to bring Shakespeare back to the West End as a commercial success.

I was, of course, always enamoured of the theatre, because my family was so closely connected with it. Henry Irving died the year after I was born, but my mother had known him from his frequent visits to her parents' house. I was fascinated by the idea that Ellen Terry and Gordon Craig were my near relations and I read all Craig's books. I had a model theatre, for which I used to design scenery, and my brother and sister and I would make up the plays together and speak the lines from behind the scenes.

I was also a tremendous fan of the ballet throughout my adolescent years. When I was àt school at Westminster my great friend was Arnold Haskell. He and I used to escape from school on our afternoons off and, in our silk top hats and tail coats, climb up to the gallery at the Coliseum to see matinées. This was just at the end of the First War. There would be one ballet in the middle of a variety programme and Diaghilev was only too glad to secure the engagement for his famous Russian dancers who had been stranded in Spain during the war. I was thrilled by the music and by Bakst's brilliant décors. I began to understand Stravinsky better and to learn a little about the technique of dancing.

I gained many of my ideas for scenery from the ballet. I could see that it was possible to have effective scenery without a lot of solidly-built sets. Diaghilev was brilliantly ahead of his time in commissioning Post-Impressionist artists like Derain, Picasso and Bérard, though his early triumphs were designed by Benois and Bakst, who were more conventional artists.

As I grew up I began to think that I would like to design scenery, because I was so taken with all the decorative arts, and I did a lot of drawing in my spare time—imaginary costumes and illustrations. I remember copying out the whole of *The Lady of Shalott* and trying to make it look like an illuminated missal. I gave it to my mother as a present. It was a very amateurish effort but it was a labour of love and took many months. I collected a whole portfolio of my drawings and, very timidly, showed one or two of them to my uncle Fred and talked about becoming a scene designer or decorator as a profession. On further enquiry, however, I discovered that I would have to learn architecture and technical drawing, and since I was hopeless at mathematics I thought, 'Oh, that's no good, I shall never be able to do that.'

I was beginning to act in a few school productions, as Mark Antony, Shylock, the Mock Turtle and Humpty Dumpty, and I did some amateur work with Rosina Filippi, a very celebrated old actress with a school in Chelsea. I also played Orlando in an open-air performance at Battle Abbey. I began to say to myself, 'What about becoming an actor?'.

My parents were not altogether enthusiastic about the theatre as a profession, though they were both enthusiastic playgoers. I tried

July 16th 1921

Dear Mr Gielgud:

I have much pleasure in informing you that Miss Helen Haye has awarded you the Scholarship (for one year's free tuition at the Benson Dramatic School). You carried off full marks (10) The thing which she makes of your performance is "natural, & unashamed" Wishing you every success

& hoping to see you at the School the opening day of the term — (Sep: 26:)

Believe me

Yours sincerely

Constance Benson—

another tack. 'Supposing you let me see if I can get into one of the dramatic schools, and then, if I haven't made a success by the time I'm twenty-five, I'll do whatever you want and go on to architecture, or try to learn proper mathematics.' I did not want to go to Oxford, even though my eldest brother Lewis was at Magdalen both before and after the First War, and my brother Val at Trinity a little later, and I had fallen in love with the city. In my last term at Westminster I had felt that I was not getting very far. I was specializing in English literature and history, and was making little progress. I knew that my grandmother and aunts had all been in the theatre from their childhood and felt it might be better to go on the stage straight away. I was seventeen.

My parents finally agreed, rather reluctantly, and I wrote to Constance Benson, Sir Frank Benson's wife, who ran a little drama school close to my grandmother's house in Cromwell Road. I recited for her and gained a scholarship. I spent a year there, playing several important roles, including scenes from *Hamlet*, Sir Peter Teazle and Benedick. There were only four or five men in the school and about twenty girls and we used to split up the parts with the slimmer girls playing young men. I seemed to be getting on quite well there, although Lady Benson—a very bad actress but a splendid teacher— thought me mannered and rather effeminate (which I was) and conceited too. She rightly put me in my place. At fhe end of each term Lady Benson used to come and act for us herself. Once she played the Ophelia mad scene in a large Edwardian hat.

And then, in 1922, my cousin Phyllis Neilson-Terry, Fred's daughter, whom I hardly knew except that I had seen her in plays and had been introduced to her in her dressing-room (I was greatly in awe of her because she was a beautiful, statuesque creature with very pale blue eyes, and a great star in those days), suddenly wrote out of the blue and asked me to go on tour with her, as assistant stage manager, understudying four parts, at a salary of £4.10s a week.

Phyllis Neilson-Terry in *The Wheel*: 'I was greatly in awe of her because she was a beautiful, statuesque creature with very pale blue eyes, and a great star in those days'

As the Poet Butterfly in *The Insect Play*, Regent, 1923.
'The Butterflies were supposed to be frightfully light-minded
creatures, all having affairs and drinking cocktails'

CHAPTER TWO

1922–1928

My grandmother Kate wrote to me of her delight that I had 'a real start in a profession you love', and added some advice. 'Don't anticipate a bed of roses for on the stage as in every other profession there are slings and arrows to contend with. Be kind and affable with all your co-mates but if possible be intimate with none of them. This is a quotation of my parents' advice to me and I pass it on as I have proved it to be very sound. Theatrical intimacy breeds jealousy of a petty kind which is very disturbing.'

Phyllis Neilson-Terry was playing a piece called *The Wheel*. In those days, London successes were usually sent on tour with less expensive casts. Edith Evans had been in the play in London, and so had Randle Ayrton and Philip Merivale, but on tour the leading man was Ion Swinley, whom I also understudied, and another actress played Miss Evans' part.

We went on a twelve- or fourteen-week tour to Hull, Leeds, Sheffield and the North, and I lived in digs, where I was constantly frightened of making a fool of myself. In the theatre I was given dogsbody jobs – seeing costumes and props out on Saturday night and in on Monday morning, checking the lights, calling Miss Terry from her dressing-room and so on.

In the last act of the play I had four lines to speak, and had to learn to make-up which I found difficult. After two hours' struggle my face would be bright orange and shiny, but the company was kind and

51

helped me, and Swinley, with whom I acted several times later, proved to be a most enchanting man. He was rather sad and lonely, I believe his wife ran off with another man when he was fighting in the First War and, embittered by this, he drank too much. I used to go on pub crawls with him from half past ten in the morning until three in the afternoon, when everyone would return to their digs, have lunch and go to sleep until the play began in the evening. That was the main form of recreation on tour in those days, when there was usually only one cinema in a town. I found it all a little disillusioning, though not in the least discouraging.

I remember once making a *faux pas* with my cousin. I knew that she had first acted under the name of Phyllida Terson (a contraction of Terry and Neilson) and one night, trying to be funny, I knocked at her door and said 'It's your call, Miss Terson.' She did not look at all pleased. I was told later that when she was called Phyllida Terson and acting with Herbert Tree, my aunt Marion, who was in the stalls, overheard somebody in the next seat saying 'Of course, she's one of Tree's illegitimate children,' so she quickly changed her acting name to Neilson-Terry. I had no idea of the gaffe which I was committing (I have become famous for dropping similar bricks), but I tried to learn to behave more carefully. 'You must never speak aloud in theatres,' I was told, 'otherwise somebody will overhear what you say and may repeat it afterwards.' However, Phyllis forgave me and she used to help me sometimes at understudy rehearsals, teaching me how to hold her—she was six feet tall—during love scenes, in case I ever had to go on, and showing me how she bent her knees and folded herself into my arms—a useful lesson.

One night I went on for one of the parts I was understudying and the company thought I did rather well. Phyllis was kind enough to say, 'When we go to Oxford your parents are coming down. I'll put you on again in that part so that they can see you.' The principal was asked to stand down, which I do not think he can have liked very much, and on I went. I was absolutely dreadful. I realized that the first time I had succeeded through sheer nerves but the second time I had no technique to rely on. One of the actors in the company told me 'I don't think you've had enough training, you ought to go to another dramatic school,' so when I came back from the tour I went to the Royal Academy of Dramatic Art and asked if I could have an audition. I won a scholarship there in 1922.

At Lady Benson's there had been only a small drill hall, and space was limited, but at the RADA there were a good many rooms. They had just opened their little theatre and it seemed very grand. The teaching was excellent. There was a lady called Alice Gachet, who taught in French and later on 'discovered' Charles Laughton, and Helen Hayes, who had, funnily enough, given me the diploma at Lady Benson's school, and Claude Rains.[1] We used to have fascinating people down to speak to us. Shaw came once, the first time I ever set eyes on him, and made a speech telling us we must never take less than £8 a week, because we would be keeping somebody else in the gutter! And Sybil Thorndike came and rehearsed us in scenes from the *Medea*.[2]

In those days Sybil had sandy hair arranged in coils round her ears, like radio receivers, and wore long, straight dresses in bright colours with strings of beads round her neck. She told me that Jason was a self-righteous prig and I must play him as such. She exuded vitality, enthusiasm, generosity and we were all spellbound as we listened to her.

I do not remember seeing her on the stage until *Saint Joan* in 1924, when I was lucky enough to be at the opening night, sitting with my parents in the dress circle of the New Theatre. It was an inspiring occasion—play, production, décor, acting, it all seemed perfect to me. At the end of the evening, when Sybil led on the weary actors, all looking utterly exhausted by the strain of the long performance, to take a dozen calls, I realized, perhaps for the first time, something of the agonies and triumphs of theatrical achievement.

Sybil Thorndike was surely the best-loved English actress since Ellen Terry, and these two great players shared many of the same fine qualities—generosity, diligence, modesty, simplicity. The theatre was the breath of life to Sybil—or rather the theatre, music and her deep religious faith. Blessed with immense talent, boundless energy, unremitting application and splendid health—until the last few years when she learned to triumph over increasing disabilities—she fought her way, helped by the devotion of a brilliant husband and loving family, to worldwide recognition. Her good works were manifold, her influence for good shone from her like a beacon, but she hated to be praised or to be thought sweet and saintly. 'I hate pathos,' she said once, 'It's soft and weak. But tragedy has fight.'

She was very fine, though to my mind unequal, in her playing of tragedy, but she was one of the few actresses of her generation who dared even to attempt it. She took the stage, whether as Lady

53

Macbeth or Queen Katharine or Hecuba, with a splendid stride, faultless phrasing and diction, and riveted her audiences with her superb authority and vocal power. In comedy she was sometimes tempted to hit too hard, but as the years passed her skill and control, under her husband Lewis Casson's iron hand, restrained and refined the execution of her art to a remarkable degree.[3]

Saint Joan, of course, was written for her, and it was her acting masterpiece, though she must have got sick and tired of hearing people say so. Her performance was unrivalled. Her tearing up of the recantation in the trial scene was a moment of really great acting that I shall never forget. She was as convincing in the slangy colloquial passages as in the great poetic speeches, blending the different sides of the character with unerring judgement, and never for a moment allowing sentimentality or sanctimoniousness to intrude on the simple directness of her approach.

In her private life she managed somehow to retain a certain reserve and dignity, despite an ebullient façade. She had beautiful manners. Genuinely interested in everyone she met, strangers as well as friends, she could bounce and flounce without ever losing her modesty and basic humility. The moment you were lucky enough to work with her in the theatre you knew she was a leader, but also a giver, not self-centred, professional to her fingertips, disciplined, punctual and kind. She confessed to having a terrible temper but I never saw a sign of it myself.

Her beauty grew, fittingly, in her old age, and her noble head, veiled in the white silk scarf she always wore, singled her out in any gathering, whether at theatres or parties or in church. During these last years, it was sad to see her the victim of continual pain. But magnificently she rose above it. 'My piffling arthritis,' she would say. With unforgettable dignity she walked at the head of her family up the long nave of Westminster Abbey, at the memorial service for her husband. Eagerly she followed every moment of the service and, typically, waited afterwards to greet a great crowd of friends. One day, soon afterwards, I called on her to find her lying in bed, evidently in great pain. 'A bit tired today,' she said, 'for it was Lewis' anniversary yesterday, so I got them to drive me up to Golders Green and sat there for half an hour.' But she announced defiantly that she intended to come to see *No Man's Land* on the following Friday. I begged her not to make the effort and thought no more about it. When the evening came, however, during the interval I heard over

the loud-speaker, above the chatter of the audience, her unmistake-
ably clear voice: 'Do you know my daughter-in-law Patricia?' Ralph
Richardson bounded into my dressing-room to tell me, 'She's here
after all!' And, of course, we both had letters from her next day.
George Devine told me that she came to see every one of the new
plays he was presenting at the Court and would always write him
vivid and constructive criticism as soon as she got home.[4]

How fitting it was that her very last public appearance should
have been at the Old Vic on its farewell night. At the end of the
performance, she was wheeled down the aisle in her chair, to smile
and wave for the last time to the people sitting in the theatre she had
always loved so well. Lively, passionate, argumentative, always
travelling, acting, learning a new language or a new poem, a magnificent wife and mother, she was surely one of the rarest women of our
time. 'Oh, Lewis,' she cried once, 'if only we could be the first actors
to play on the moon.'

After the excitement of the *Medea* and Sybil Thorndike, we did a very
ambitious play which Claude Rains directed—*The Living Corpse*. It is
a highly elaborate piece, with a huge cast, about a man who leaves
his wife, goes to live with the gypsies and then disappears. The wife
marries again, and the police find the husband in a low dive and
arrest him for bigamy. In the last scene he appears with a straggling
beard, wearing nothing under his huge overcoat, falls at his wife's
feet to beg her forgiveness, and finally shoots himself—all tremendously Russian and melodramatic.

Rains suggested that I should take the leading role of Fedya. We
borrowed all the props, rehearsed like mad and learned to sing the
gypsy songs. The performance was quite a success in the end, though
I cannot imagine how I had the courage to take on such an ambitious
part. Nigel Playfair, who was a friend of my mother's, came to see me
in one of the public shows.[5] He liked it and offered me a part in *The
Insect Play*, by the Čapek brothers, which he was putting on at the
Regent Theatre.

In *The Insect Play* I had a most embarrassing part. The first act was
entitled 'The Butterflies', the second act 'The Beetles', the third 'The
Ants'. The second and third acts were splendid, but the first was a
disaster. In the original production in Czechoslovakia this act had

55

apparently been highly improper, concerned mainly with fornication. The Butterflies were frightfully light-minded creatures, having affairs, drinking cocktails, and so on. Playfair and Clifford Bax, who adapted the play, tried to alter this first act, removing the indecencies, and the result was very tame indeed. I played the Poet Butterfly, and looked terrible in a laurel wreath, white flannels and pumps. I had to come on with a battledore and shuttlecock which I failed to aim correctly. On the last night Playfair sat in a box with his back to the stage all through the first act, which depressed us very much.

As a producer Playfair was unobtrusive. I remember nothing he said, but once when I was sitting behind him at a dress rehearsal, I made a most impertinent suggestion. But he turned round and said, 'It's a very good idea, I will do that.' He had no side at all. His manners were charming and he was very easy-going. It was said that when there was a crisis, he invariably walked out of the theatre and went for a stroll until his manager had dealt with the situation. Easy-going he may have been, but he had great integrity. He was rather tubby, short-sighted, smoked an enormous pipe and wore very shabby clothes. He loved to stay at Oxford, at the inn at Godstow, and bathe in the river. He had an extraordinary flair for the eighteenth century. His production of *The Beggars' Opera* at the Lyric, Hammersmith, was enchantingly pretty, too pretty perhaps, as the squalid satire of the play was lost—Playfair's highwaymen and doxies were rogues in porcelain. But how wonderfully well he did it.

The Lyric Theatre at Hammersmith—recently rebuilt—was a beautiful old Victorian house which had been shut for ages. There was a butcher's shop alongside the theatre which stank in hot weather, and all the local boys used to bang on the dock doors with hoop sticks and make a fearful racket. It was uncomfortable and smelly, the dressing-rooms were wretched, but it had a unique atmosphere.

The Regent was an important theatre for me in my early career, as I appeared in three productions there, though they were all unsuccessful. When *The Insect Play* ended its six-week run there, Playfair decided to put on a chronicle history play called *Robert E. Lee*, a sequel to *Abraham Lincoln*, by John Drinkwater. *Lincoln* had been an enormous success but the sequel, which was rather long drawn out, was less satisfactory. However, Playfair engaged a huge company of twenty-five and asked me to play Lee's aide-de-camp. I was

56

Sir Nigel Playfair on the stage of the Lyric, Hammersmith (by George Belcher). Right: A scene from his production of *The Insect Play*

No greater name than Nigel Playfair
Occurs in Thespian lore or myth;
'Twas he who first revealed to Mayfair
The whereabouts of Hammersmith.

dreadfully bad. I walked clumsily, could not manage my boots, tripped over my sword, and was thoroughly ashamed of myself. But I was also understudying Claude Rains who played one of the other leading parts. Rains seemed to like me and encouraged me. I had always been enormously impressed by his acting. He had been in Henry Ainley's companies in 1918 and 1919 at the St James's and afterwards went to the Everyman in Hampstead, where he acted a lot of Shaw — Napoleon in *The Man of Destiny,* and Dubedat in *The Doctor's Dilemma.* In both those parts he was splendid, so when I went to the Regent and found I was to understudy him, I was naturally thrilled. He was ill one day and I went on for two or three performances and seemed to do quite well. I was lucky to get the chance of playing but as a result I tended to become imitative. I had little idea at that time of playing a part with any originality.

At the end of 1923, after leaving RADA, I played Charles Wykeham, one of the dreadful boys in *Charley's Aunt,* at the Comedy Theatre. Even though I thought it would be rather fun to be in a farce, I did not enjoy it. Amy Brandon-Thomas, the daughter of the author, was determined that the play should be done exactly as it had been from the very beginning, a kind of tradition, like Gilbert and Sullivan.

In 1924 J. B. Fagan sent for me to his house in St John's Wood and asked me if I would like to go to Oxford and play six or seven parts in a repertory season there. He had taken a curious place in Woodstock Road, an archaeological museum full of stuffed animals, known locally as the Red Barn. The seats were bentwood chairs ranged on wooden planks so that when you moved the whole row shifted and squeaked. There was no front curtain, and we never knew where to put the prompter whom we always needed very badly because, as we did a new play every week, we all used to dry up and make mistakes. It was an ambitious programme, but great fun. I lived in Oxford in a tiny flat in the High and earned £8 a week, a marvellous sum to me in those days.

The indefatigable Richard Goolden was in the company and Flora Robson as well. Tyrone Guthrie was also a member of the company and tried to act — not very successfully — but he was very amusing and an original personality. I played three seasons at Oxford and had some very good parts and in 1924 I did my first — silent — film: *Who is the Man?* playing a dope-fiend sculptor in a part originally written for Sarah Bernhardt.

Sir Tyrone Guthrie. He began his career with me at Oxford in 1924, but J. B. Fagan persuaded him he would never succeed as an actor so he became a director, first in radio and later in the theatre all over the world

Left: Noël Coward as Lewis Dodd in *The Constant Nymph*, directed by Basil Dean in 1926, and (below) myself in the same part later that season

At the end of the first Oxford season Fagan released me to go to understudy Noël Coward, who was playing Nicky Lancaster in his first success *The Vortex.*⁶ Someone had said 'Oh, I hear you play the piano a bit,' which is why I got the job (and why I got the job in *The Constant Nymph* afterwards). In fact, I can only play by ear, like my father, and have never been able to read music.

I went to see Noël at the Royalty Theatre in Dean Street, very apprehensive of course, but very thrilled to meet him. His dressing-room was full of bottles of Chanel No. 5, with twenty dressing-gowns in the wardrobe. He had just finished writing a revue for Cochran called *On With the Dance,* which was shortly to be produced in Manchester and Noël wanted to go up for the first night to see it, so he said I should take over Nicky Lancaster for that performance. It was my first smart, West End engagement. A few weeks later Noël decided to leave the cast to have a holiday before taking the play to New York, and Lilian Braithwaite very kindly agreed to forego her holiday and continue in the play while I succeeded Noël. We were acting at the Little Theatre in John Street, Adelphi one night, when a cat came on to the stage while we were playing the big emotional scene in the last act. I became so hysterical that I threw it into the audience. Fortunately the auditorium was almost level with the stage, and the cat was able to slip away.

I was very much aware that Noël was an infinitely better Nicky Lancaster than I was. It was a highly-strung, nervous, hysterical part which depended a lot upon emotion. I found it tiring to play because I did not know how to save myself. However, the play ran a long time and did good business, which was rather gratifying at that stage in my career.

Noël was always word-perfect at the first rehearsal and expected the whole company to be the same. This was all very well for him because he was usually the author too. He had terrible rows with Gladys Cooper and Edith Evans in later years because they would not learn his lines beforehand. He used to say that it wasted so much time. In my view, it is much easier to learn the words when you have the movements and the business. It is important to know how the other actor is going to speak his line so that both of you can react properly. If you start absolutely word-perfect, like a parrot, I think it makes everything flat and dull. Perhaps Noël's method suited his own plays – they are written in a very clipped, staccato style, and he nearly always played them with people like Gertrude Lawrence, an

Right: Trofimov in *The Cherry Orchard*, Oxford 1925. 'I made up to look like my brother Val' (below)

extraordinary, volatile, talented creature who invariably gave the plays a rhythm and quality of her own. She was a much greater actress than Noël was an actor, though he too was highly skilled and spoke his own words and lyrics quite brilliantly, with marvellous pace and diction.

Noël was always highly professional and very much down on anybody who was not. He adored Hawtrey, who, he said, had taught him everything he knew. Hawtrey fascinated me too. I saw him in a number of plays, and he never seemed to do anything at all. He was fat, with a lazy manner, not good-looking at all, but with impeccable timing – and a deadpan perfection in comic situations.

I went back to Oxford for the 1924–5 season. Fagan put on *The Cherry Orchard*, which had then not been seen in England except in a Stage Society production when many of the audience walked out through sheer boredom. We were all bewildered by the play, but I found the part of the student Trofimov fascinating. I thought I would make up with a bald wig and steel spectacles – Chekhov says that the student's hair is very thin. When I walked on to the stage at the first performance, I suddenly thought, 'This isn't what I thought acting was. I'm just part of a novel, or a family, or something very intimate, and I don't care what they feel about it in front, I know I have to do it this way.' It was a revelation to me. I also began to see, for the first time, that it was possible to project a personality completely different from one's own, rather than just showing off.

Although none of us understood the play there was an extraordinary sincerity about the performance, and a feeling of discovery for the young company. When Playfair came to see it he immediately offered to transfer it to the Lyric, Hammersmith, where we had a rapturous first night followed by a very mixed press. Playfair decided it was a failure and engaged a cast for a revival of *The Beggars' Opera* to replace it. But Fagan decided to move us to the Royalty Theatre in Dean Street and we ran there all through the summer. It was a great success and, for me, a thrilling engagement because it led to so many things afterwards.

In 1924, I played my first Romeo in London with Gwen Ffrangcon-Davies.[7] She had seen me in *The Insect Play* and thought I was simply awful, and when she heard I was to play Romeo she practically had a fit. Fortunately at the first rehearsal she took a fancy to me and we have been devoted friends from that day to this. She had had a very exciting career, mostly in Birmingham, as Barry

Jackson's leading lady.[8] She made her greatest success as Elizabeth Browning in *The Barretts of Wimpole Street,* but to my mind, Jackson never really exploited her potential. He was not certain that he wanted stars in his company; he believed in a repertory company— which is perhaps why I got the part of Romeo.

Gwen played everything with extraordinary skill and wit. When she played the subordinate part of Lady Herbert in *The Lady with the Lamp*, a play about Florence Nightingale with Edith Evans in the main part, she almost surpassed Edith. Both characters had to age during the course of the action and Gwen's old lady in the last act was particularly moving.

She was always wonderfully kind to me. I was only nineteen when I played Romeo with her and from the start she taught and encouraged me. She set such a good example, never playing the spoilt leading lady, even though the costumes were clumsily made and she was sewing her own dresses in the wardrobe twenty-four hours before the curtain went up. At the dress rehearsal we were both so full of pins we could hardly embrace. I had no say, of course, in how I was to look, and had to suffer a black wig with a centre parting and white tights with soles sewn onto them—very difficult to move in. Romeo is a very long and arduous part and I was no good at the sword-fights. Scott Sunderland, one of Jackson's favourite actors, was playing Mercutio in a very violent style. He used to knock me about on the stage which made me nervous and threw me off balance. I spoke the lines not too badly, I think, but I was so inexperienced that it must have been very hard on Gwen.

Gwen and I were engaged, at a rather large salary for those days, to do the balcony scene from *Romeo and Juliet* for two or three weeks at the Coliseum with top billing. We were given a terrible set, with a sort of cardboard pink marble balcony. Gwen looked as if she was standing in a pink bath when she appeared and the audience did not know what to make of it. The scene went very badly, but one of the stagehands was kind enough to say to me during the last week, 'You're doing it a bit better now'. The Houston sisters used to follow us and we were preceded by a huge man called Teddy Brown. He weighed about twenty stone and played the xylophone. He was such a success with the audience that when the revolve began to go round they were still screaming for him as our garden scene was heaving into view. And when the Houston sisters came on, one of them would give a sort of imitation of me with her Scotch accent—'A thousand

Above: Romeo to Gwen Ffrangcon-Davies' Juliet, Regent 1924

Right: Oswald in Ibsen's *Ghosts*, with Mrs Patrick Campbell as Mrs Alving, matinée performances at Wyndham's, 1928 times goodnight' — and get a huge laugh. It was the only time I have ever appeared in a music hall.

The year 1928 was the centenary of Ibsen's birth and I was asked to play in a revival of *Ghosts* with Mrs Patrick Campbell.[9] I had seen her many years before on tour in Croydon in *Mrs Tanqueray* and she had had a tremendous effect on me, although she was fat and middle-aged. I saw her again in *Pygmalion*, in a revival, with my Aunt Marion as Mrs Higgins, and also in *The Matriarch*, which was one of her last successes. She could sulk on the stage in a way that was perfect for Eliza Doolittle and for Hedda Gabler as well. She could be beguiling, casual, wayward, petulant and disagreeable, yet manage to be glamorous at the same time.

When I played with her in *Ghosts* we gave only matinées and hardly anybody came. Mrs Campbell was very cross that the house was so poor and that none of her Society friends had bothered to turn up. She dearly loved a Lord. She would say to me out loud during a scene, 'the Marquis and Marchioness of Empty are in front again!' She was an extraordinary, fascinating woman, and we became great friends. I was very flattered that she seemed to like me, because I knew how difficult she was. She was losing her friends and she had hardly any money, though she refused to take any notice of that. She was defiant about her unpopularity both with managers and actors who appeared with her. She had had two unhappy marriages, and her love affairs, such as they were, were not very successful. She could have been a great director. She was wonderful at rehearsals, and I believe she had taught du Maurier a great deal. He was in her company some years before, though she was supposed to have said, 'Oh, how can I act with a dreadful, ugly face like that?' She could be wise and even affectionate and why she had to be so ill-behaved, sometimes even common and rude, it was difficult to tell. A kind of demon seized her and she could not resist being unkind to people, making cheap jokes at their expense. Yet she could also be witty, very ladylike and gracious.

When I was first asked to her flat in Pont Street I expected to find a gypsy atmosphere. On the contrary, there were Morris wallpapers, a bust of Dante with flowers in front of it and a beautiful grand piano. She had been a great idol of the Pre-Raphaelites and Beardsley once made a wonderful sketch of her. From the time I first met her, in 1928, until her death during the Second War, I saw her quite a lot, both in England and America, and I became enormously fond of her.

I once took months trying to find a play for her and thought I had succeeded. The part was tailor-made for her, an ex-opera singer who took pupils in a mountain chalet. Throughout the first act she was making pasta, occasionally obliging with excerpts from her opera triumphs. In the third act there was a scene in which her daughter was being stoned because she had had an affair with a peasant and went into a church for refuge. She put on the Madonna's robe and crown and the peasants thought she was the Mother of God come to life and knelt down and worshipped her. In the next act the daughter returned home and her mother had to say, 'I salute my genius in you', and fall on her knees. I thought this would be the most marvellous scene for Mrs Campbell, but she only said sulkily, 'I suppose you want me to play the daughter.' She was then about seventy and extremely fat. It was preposterous, but typical of the way she cut the ground from under your feet, so you could not help her or advise her.

When we played together in *Ghosts*, James Agate[10] said she was like the Lord Mayor's coach with nothing in it! Indeed, she did very little with the part, being far too busy insulting the unfortunate man playing Pastor Manders. He was frightened to death of her and sweated furiously. She would say with her back to the audience, 'Oh, look at that old man with the sweat pouring onto his stomach.' In the great scene where I had to tell her that I had got brain disease she taught me most carefully how to say my line ('The disease I suffer from is seated here' – pointing to my forehead). She said, 'You must speak with a channel-steamer voice. Pinero showed me how to do it!' As I was preparing to say the line at the first performance, she said, in a loud aside, 'Oh, I am so hungry!' Yet, at the dress rehearsal, when one would have expected her to be most difficult, she had sailed through, knowing every line and being most impressive. She was totally unpredictable. Later on I started to direct her in a play by Rodney Ackland, *Strange Orchestra*, in which she would have been wonderful. She rehearsed for two weeks and then threw up the part because her dog was in quarantine. She used to draw funny pictures of everybody during rehearsals.

Rehearsing *Pygmalion* with Tree she must have been impossible. They were both such eccentrics. They kept ordering each other out of the theatre with Shaw in the middle, trying to cope with them. How the play ever came out I cannot imagine. I saw the revival in which she played Eliza again – she was fifty in 1914 when she first created the part. She was far too old, of course, but she did some wonderful things. I remember her knitting in the last act, very haughtily, speaking with a terrible bogus accent. She was brilliant in the tea scene. I have an idea that Shaw wrote it as a skit on her real voice, the booming contralto that everybody used to love to imitate.

When I went to see her in *The Matriarch*, she played the last act in a wheelchair wearing a big fur cloak, and a black hat with a veil. At the end of the performance—I knew how to get backstage because I had played in that theatre—I pushed the pass-door open and said, 'Where's Mrs Campbell's dressing-room?' 'Oh, she's gone,' they said. 'Gone, how can she have? She was taking her call a minute ago.' 'Oh, she always goes out with the audience, just drops her cloak in the wings and pushes past them.'

I saw her play Ella Rentheim in *John Gabriel Borkman* in a little repertory theatre at Kew Bridge. Her dressing-room was so small that she could hardly move in it. She gave a marvellous performance in the second and fourth acts, and a disgraceful one in the other two. Mrs Borkman was played by an actress called Nancy Price whom Mrs Campbell disliked. They refused to take any notice of one another, which was something of a drawback since the first act consists almost entirely of a duologue between Mrs Borkman and Ella Rentheim. The two ladies sat in large armchairs on either side of the stage (with two prompters as near as possible in the wings) looking straight into the audience, and speaking their lines without taking any notice of each other at all. Then the second act began. Mrs Campbell liked Victor Lewisohn, who played Borkman, and thought him a fine actor. So she suddenly blossomed and gave the most wonderful performance. She only acted to please herself, with no sense of responsibility towards an audience or her fellow actors. Yet she came to see me act quite often and used to give me wonderful tips. When I was playing *Hamlet* in New York she sent me a card—'Give me the beauty I long for'. I asked my director to invite her to the party after the performance and she behaved with appalling tactlessness. She went up to Judith Anderson, who was playing the Queen, and said, 'Why do you sit on the bed? Only housemaids sit on the bed!' To the director, she said, 'Why has the ghost got mumps?' (The ghost wore a large mask.)

I was with her in New York the day Edward VIII abdicated. We had just been to see Charles Laughton in the film *Rembrandt*. When we came out, the famous Abdication speech from Fort Belvedere was being broadcast. We went into the Plaza Hotel to hear it. Mrs Campbell burst into tears and said, 'Let's send him a telegram.' I suggested that since we did not know the ex-King and in any case he would have left Fort Belvedere by this time, it was not a good idea. 'Oh, yes, we must, we must,' she said, so we rushed to a post office.

She said to the clerk, 'Isn't this wonderful? The greatest thing since Antony gave up a kingdom for Cleopatra.' The woman took a piece of gum out of her mouth and replied, 'Oh, I guess he just wanted to go play ball.' I finally persuaded her to send a telegram to Charles Laughton instead, saying how much we had enjoyed his film.

It was in the early 1920s that the Guitrys, father and son, first appeared in London with their enchanting leading lady, Yvonne Printemps.[11] I have a vivid recollection of Lucien Guitry's acting in a drama called *Jacqueline*, produced in London in 1922, in which he played an elderly roué who strangles his mistress in the final scene. It was the preparation for this denouement in the second act that impressed me most. The scene was in a hotel bedroom where he had taken the girl for a weekend. Guitry stood over her as she lay on the bed, and she suddenly shrank from him crying, 'Oh! You terrify me.' For a few seconds he seemed to grow inches taller and become a towering and sadistic creature. Then, suddenly breaking the tension completely, he resumed his normally charming manner for the rest of the scene. I watched him most intently, and am convinced that in fact he did absolutely nothing, not moving his hands, his face or his body. His absolute stillness and the projection of his concentrated imagination, controlled and executed with a consummate technique, produced on the girl and on the audience an extraordinary and unforgettable effect. I knew I had seen a great actor.

I met Sacha Guitry on only one occasion. In March 1939 Peggy Ashcroft and I were invited to appear at a gala given in the courtyard at the Foreign Office to celebrate the state visit of the French President, M. Lebrun. It was a tremendous affair, the last of its kind before the war, and I could not help referring to it afterwards as the Duchess of Richmond's Ball. There was a magnificent profusion of flowers, sent from Sir Philip Sassoon's garden at Lympne, masses of azaleas edging the balconies, and a positive thicket of madonna lilies dividing the stage from the auditorium.

Sacha Guitry had been invited to appear with Seymour Hicks in a sketch written by them both. Hicks was a great admirer of Sacha and had acted in English versions of several of his plays. The humour of the little piece was supposed to lie in attempts by Sacha to speak English and Hicks to reply in French. Both actors were exceedingly nervous and obviously under-rehearsed. I watched them from the wings as they kept drying up and killing each other's laughs, which were not very plentiful in any case. Appearing with them was Sacha's latest wife, Geneviève Sereville, an extremely young and pretty girl. At the morning rehearsal Peggy and I had been asked to be introduced to the distinguished visitors. Mlle Sereville was dressed in a very short skirt, and her stockings were rolled below the knees like a footballer's, showing a considerable expanse of thigh. We stammered a few polite words in our somewhat halting French, to which M. Guitry, an imposing figure with fur collar and gold-topped cane, made suitably gracious acknowledgement. As we moved away to find our dressing-rooms I ventured to remark to Hicks 'I say, sir, that's a remarkably attractive girl with M. Guitry, don't you think?' and was rewarded by the trenchant comment, 'Try acting with her, old boy. It's the cabman's goodbye.'

The first time I saw my name in lights was in 1928 in a farce with Hermione Baddeley. It was an appalling concoction, backed by the lady who had written it, called *Holding Out the Apple*. It contained, among many others, one immortal line: 'You've got a way of holding out the apple that positively gives me the pip.' It ran about six weeks, largely to an audience of nurses in free seats. I was next to play in a ghastly thriller called *The Skull*, and later in another drama, *Out of the Sea* at the Strand Theatre, in which I played a pianist who strummed excerpts from *Tristan* on the piano before committing suicide with the heroine on a rock. That was a disaster too. I began to feel restive. It was agreeable to be well paid, announced in big letters at the top of the bill, but not in such wretched plays. Then I had a chance to replace Leslie Banks in *The Lady With the Lamp* with Edith Evans and Gwen Ffrangcon-Davies.

I had never worked with Edith Evans before, but I had seen her in a number of plays and admired her enormously. We rehearsed our scenes together — I was very much in awe of her — and she kept saying that I was not *dirty* enough in the scene when I was carried in, dying on a stretcher. To make myself dirtier I used to strip in the dressing-room and cover myself with fuller's earth, so that when she touched me in the hospital scene she would believe that I was encrusted with the dust of the battlefield.

Sybil Thorndike seemed to revel in her success, but Edith Evans did not. Edith was undoubtedly the greater artist of the two; Sybil was the greater woman. Edith Evans was the finest actress of our time and I am privileged to have known and worked with her so often. She was not always easy. There was something rather aloof about her. She was not a cosy person, except when you could get her alone occasionally. In Bryan Forbes' life of her she told him that she liked me only when we were alone together, away from all the frivolous nonsense with which I liked to surround myself. I admired her dedication. She was not gregarious, and she found it difficult to open out to people. Like Ellen Terry and Peggy Ashcroft she longed to be an ordinary woman, to have a home, a husband, perhaps children. She never had them. At different times she tried to take up dancing, farming, attempted to drive a car or skate, to do the everyday things that an ordinary woman does. But she was always driven back to the theatre — just as Ellen Terry was.

She had been first discovered by the eccentric William Poel, who cast her as Cressida, after rehearsing her first in several male parts in the same production. He had encouraged her to leave the Belgravia hat-shop in which she had been working and become a professional actress.[12] At that time she was considered plain, and leading ladies were expected to be beautiful. Edith Evans was no beauty in the conventional sense. Her eyes, with their heavy lids, were set with one slightly lower than the other, giving her face an enigmatic originality. But it was a fascinating canvas on which she soon learned to paint any character she chose. I remember once saying as a young actor 'I would love a photograph of Edith Evans. I never know what she looks like, she always looks like the part.' It was probably the greatest compliment I could have paid her.

It was as Millamant, in Congreve's *The Way of the World*, that she took the town by storm. It was a unique and exquisite performance. She purred and challenged, mocked and melted, showing her changing moods by subtly shifting the angles of her head, neck and shoulders. Poised and cool, like a porcelain figure in a vitrine, she used her fan—which she never opened—in the great love scene as an instrument for attack or defence, now coquettishly pointing it upwards beneath her chin, now resting it languidly against her cheek. Her words flowed on, phrasing and diction balanced in perfect cadences, as she smiled and pouted in delivering her delicious sallies. She displayed her superb taste by perfect timing and control, never stooping to indulge an over-enthusiastic audience, and disdaining any temptation to overstress an emotional moment or allow too many laughs to interrupt the pace of a comic scene.

She grew to hate her success as Lady Bracknell, though it was perhaps the most popular and famous of all her great impersonations. She was staying at my cottage in Essex one weekend just before the War when I suggested a possible revival of the Wilde play. I took a copy from the bookshelf and we read the handbag scene together to the other guests. After the laughter had died down Edith handed me back the book and remarked gravely, 'I know those sort of women. They ring the bell and tell you to put a lump of coal on the fire.'

She disliked the imitations of her trumpet tone in the famous line 'A *handbag?*' which many people seemed to think was the alpha and omega of her performance as Lady Bracknell. For me there was so much else to admire. There were the exquisite details of observation and execution; the sly look of suspicion, for instance, as she glanced at the armchair she had chosen for the interview with Worthing in the first act. In those few seconds she managed to convey both appraisal and approval, as if reassuring herself of the suitability of that particular piece of furniture as a throne for her corseted dignity, before deigning to lower herself into the seat. She strove to create her performances from an inner conviction, trying to find the 'bridges', as she called them, to achieve progression and climax in the characters she was determined to bring to life. 'I never make effects,' she used to say. Of course she did—but with what subtlety, skill and artistry.

In 1932 I was asked to direct—for the first time in that capacity—a production of *Romeo and Juliet* at Oxford for the OUDS,* and was enriched by the privilege of working with Peggy Ashcroft as Juliet and Edith Evans as the Nurse. Of course, I was greatly in awe of Edith at first. I timidly suggested that she might perhaps be doing needlework in her opening scene with Juliet and Lady Capulet. I pictured her, I suppose, with a tapestry in a frame and a large needle

*Oxford University Dramatic Society

threading in and out, typical romantic costume-play 'business'. I was quite wrong, though she knew at once what I was driving at. She kept a tiny piece of material between her hands which she handled very sparingly (almost hiding it in her long sleeves) using a gentle rhythmic movement to give a slight counterpoint to her first long speech without in the least detracting from it. It was my first glimpse of her remarkable instinct for selectivity.

She preferred to move very little. I do not remember any swift entrances or exits in her performances and she taught me to give up my own impatient inclination to drive actors about the stage in order to give a scene excitement long before the dialogue demanded it. You could not hurry Edith or muddle her with too many suggestions before she was ready for them. The character and its truth, the pattern of the syllables, the give and take of the vocal exchanges, these were slowly taking shape during the early rehearsals and from these basic foundations she began to develop her performance. Not until the part really began to possess her would she completely sweep in to her performance. She could not, as some actors do, patch together old material which she had tried out successfully in other plays in order to achieve a superficial short cut to a new creation.

She was always extremely reticent about the acting of her colleagues; praise from her was as precious as it was rare. Once she paid me a sublime compliment which I shall always cherish. 'Your Benedick, Johnnie,' she said after a rather stormy argument about the playing of comedy, 'that performance, you know, was seven-eighths perfection!'

CHAPTER
THREE

1929–1930

At the end of 1928 I suddenly had an offer from Harcourt Williams, whom I knew slightly, to go to the Old Vic.[1] I was reluctant to go because of the salary, which was only £10 a week. As a sort of leading man I was being paid about £50 a week in the West End and getting billed above the title. Harcourt Williams was offering me a season with several leads, though none specified in the contract. In two minds whether to accept or not, I went to Edith Evans between performances of *The Lady with the Lamp*. Usually she never saw anybody while she was resting, but she asked me in and gave me a long talk, and finally said, 'If you want to learn how to play Shakespeare, I think you'd be very wise to accept it.' And so I did.

Martita Hunt was engaged to play opposite me and Gyles Isham, who had been a very successful Hamlet as an undergraduate at Oxford, was also in the company. Lilian Baylis thought that he would probably play it again at the Vic.[2] When it came to discussing parts and I said I wanted to play Hamlet, she hedged and havered, though finally I did get the part. After a few weeks, I found that I got on well with the company, especially with Harcourt Williams, though not with Donald Wolfit, who always disliked me very much. In fact, when he was afterwards in management, with a great reputation in Shakespeare, he referred to me as 'the Enemy' and used to go purple in the face at the very mention of my name. He was a powerful actor, who had learned his business from Matheson Lang

My first *Hamlet*, the Old Vic, 1929/30

A woodcut by Powell Lloyd of me as Prospero in
The Tempest, Old Vic 1930

My first Richard II, Old Vic 1929: 'I could see from the company's attitude that they all thought I was going
to be good'

and Fred Terry, but had also learned some of their old-fashioned actor-manager's tricks, and he lacked any sense of humour, particularly about himself. He was jealous too, and though often effective, could, I thought, be very tasteless in his acting.

Harcourt Williams was a delightful man. He was a vegetarian and carried around a big tin of Bemax to keep him going. His devoted wife, who was a diseuse and gave recitals every year for children, adored him and was always at his right hand to encourage him. He was a very modest man. He had been with Ellen Terry, Benson and Granville-Barker and had an enormous admiration for them all. He had been a very good actor himself, and extremely good-looking, too, as a young man. But he was beginning to age during the two arduous Vic seasons of 1929–31 and he tired very easily. As soon as he found he could get on so well with me and with Martita—and in the second season with Ralph Richardson and Leslie French—he would invite us to go and have buns with him at lunchtime and would ask us for suggestions. I would rough out ideas for sets and Ralph for casting, and we were all encouraged to contribute and have our say.

I had walked on at the Old Vic right back in 1921 as an unpaid student between terms at the Benson school. In those days the company had been full of the sort of old actors you read about in Dickens. I was terrified of them because they were real old 'laddies', rushing off to the bar every five minutes and using awful language. I walked on there in four plays in which Russell Thorndike played all the leads, Hamlet, Peer Gynt, Wat Tyler and Lear, four huge parts in the space of five weeks. He knew them all perfectly and acted with great wit and drive. My first speaking part was the Herald in *Henry V* with one line—'Here is the number of the slaughter'd French.'

In 1929 my first role was to be Romeo and, just as before, it was not a success. Adele Dixon played Juliet and Wolfit was Mercutio. Williams tried to make us play very fast in order to get through the whole play in the two hours that the Chorus says it should last. The result was that we gabbled and the audience could barely hear us. This was Williams' first attempt to carry out the instructions in Granville-Barker's prefaces.

Next we did *The Merchant of Venice*, in which I played Antonio and Brember Wills was not very successful as Shylock. Then we did a version of Molière's *Le Malade Imaginaire*, and after that *Richard II*. I could see from the company's attitude that they all thought I was going to be good in *Richard II* and I felt elated at being allowed to play the part. It ran for only about three weeks and there were hardly any notices, but I began to feel I had made a real personal success.

This was, in fact, one of the advantages of the Vic. A young actor could try his wings without being slanged or over-praised the next day. I played Macbeth later on in that first season and James Agate came to one of the matinées, representing the great *Sunday Times*. He came round to my dressing room after the murder scene and said 'You were very good in that scene, but I know you can't do the rest of the play so I just thought I would come round and tell you now!' But mostly the critics did not come at all, and we depended for success on the loyal Vic audience.

The audiences at the Vic were very lively. There was an old lady called Miss Pilgrim who ran a stationer's shop in Islington. She had been a fan of the Old Vic for years and used to walk all the way from Islington to Waterloo Road for the first nights and many other performances. She always sat in the gallery and at the end of the performance she would sing 'God Save the King' in a very loud cracked voice. She had a wall eye, we all knew her by sight and she used to write letters to us. A year or two after I had left, when Tyrone Guthrie took over the direction, stars like Charles Laughton, Athene Seyler, Flora Robson and James Mason were in the company. Miss Pilgrim went to the stage door one night and asked everybody in the company to sign their autographs for her as they came out of the theatre. The next day they found that the paper had been folded over, and on the other side she had written a demand to the Governors that Tyrone Guthrie should be sacked.

I doubt whether Lilian Baylis had any real understanding of Shakespeare. In fact, I do not think she ever saw a play right through. I would meet her wandering about the passages during performances or she would write letters behind a curtain in the back of her box. But she always seemed to know exactly what was happening in her theatre. She never involved herself in rows over productions, apart from the invariable comment that it was all costing too much. She liked coming on to the stage herself in her cap and gown, and making rather jolly appeals to the public, telling them that they must all come to the theatre much more and that they were all bounders. She was a parochial mother-figure, but with this extraordinary belief that she was there for a purpose which it was her duty to carry out. Her opening of Sadler's Wells at the beginning of the thirties, for instance, was madness. The theatre was horrible, done up

Richard II in my own production of Shakespeare's play, Queen's 1937

as cheaply as possible with very poor acoustics. We all dreaded it.

Our production of *Hamlet* that 1929–30 season had been so success-
ful that Maurice Browne, who was then a producer—he had put on
Journey's End and made a lot of money—transferred it to the Queen's
Theatre in the West End. That was where I crossed swords with
Wolfit. He was playing the King, and thought I had influenced
Williams to cut his part for the West End, which of course I had not.
But he grumbled and groused throughout the run. The weather was
appallingly hot that summer and by some extraordinary chance
Henry Ainley was playing *Hamlet* at the Haymarket and Alexander
Moissi was playing it in German at the Globe, so there were three
Hamlets in the West End together.

The Globe was next door and I went to a matinée to see the
production. Moissi had a curious tenor voice. He was playing, of
course, in German which I could not understand, but although I
knew the part by heart I was unable to follow the text. There were
some impressive things in the production, but Moissi himself was a
very poor Hamlet. He appeared to be permanently sorry for himself,
crying into his handkerchief in the Nunnery scene, and finally stab-
bing the King in the back. I was introduced to him backstage and he
looked me up and down and said, through his interpreter, 'Oh, you
play it in the Spanish style, I see.' (My costume had a high white
collar and black trunk hose). That was all he said. He was wearing a
costume that somehow combined Peter Pan with the Middle Ages,
and it did not suit him very well. But I also saw him as Fedya in *The
Living Corpse* and thought him strikingly effective in it.

I was not thought of as a character actor in those days, having so
often played nervous, hysterical young men. But I had a feeling that
perhaps if I played a character with truth it might make me a better
actor. In juvenile parts I was inclined to be an exhibitionist and for a
long time my ambition was to be frightfully smart and West End,
wear beautifully cut suits lounging on sofas in French window
comedies. The Vic began to cure me of such ideas. When I was asked
to play Hamlet, the great juvenile part of all times, at first I thought I
would make a terrible hash of it because I felt I could give only an
inferior copy of the other Hamlets I had seen—about twelve by that
time. At drama school I had loved trailing my black cloak around,
posing and being emotional, but I had a feeling there was something
wrong with that.

I threw myself into the part like a man learning to swim and I found that the text would hold me up if I sought the truth in it. It occurred to me that most actors tried to whitewash the unpleasant aspects of Hamlet's character. The handsome, middle-aged stars of the Edwardian theatre romanticized the part. Even John Barrymore, whose Hamlet I admired very much, cut the play outrageously so that he could, for instance, play the closet scene all out for sentiment, with the emphasis on the 'Oedipus complex' – sobbing on Gertrude's bosom. Yet Barrymore, like Russell Thorndike, had a wonderful edge and a demonic sense of humour. Ernest Milton had the same quality. Of all the actors in my time I felt he must be the nearest to Irving, with the same kind of extravagance and flowery, sinister power.

The majority of people who remember my Hamlet saw it at the Haymarket Theatre in 1944, the last time I played it in London. But the few people alive who saw both my last and my first Hamlet say that the Old Vic version was the better. To see a Hamlet aged twenty-five was a new experience for the public then. The actors in the Edwardian period never played it until they were forty – John Barrymore was forty-five when I saw him. The youthful tantrums and despair of the opening scenes were perhaps more poignant because I was so young. And then, as I have said, I tried to find the violent and ugly colours in the part.[3]

In the 1944 production, which George Rylands directed, I felt I was too old to get the same effects in the opening scenes, though I was perhaps better in the last ones. Harley Granville-Barker had given me a great many valuable notes about the play when we did the Elsinore production just before the war.

In 1945 I played Hamlet for the troops in the Middle East, which was exciting because there were no critics to worry about and success or failure was unimportant. What mattered was to make them listen by trying to do it as well as possible. The trouble with the Rylands production was that I was too tired. We were performing three other plays in repertory with two performances on Wednesdays and Saturdays. At the matinée I would sleep on my sofa for ten minutes during Ophelia's mad scene, which is the only wait Hamlet has, and after the final curtain would swallow a cup of tea and start making up for the evening performance.

The most thrilling Hamlet for me was the production in New York in 1936, because I felt I was on my mettle. It was my first big chance in America, and I was presented by an American management with

Above: Hamlet, with Martita Hunt as Gertrude, Old Vic, 1929/30 'To see a Hamlet of twenty-five was a new experience for the public then'

Left: As Hotspur with Dorothy Green (Lady Percy) and Lilian Baylis, at the inaugural party for the re-opening of Sadler's Wells, 1931

Right: Hamlet in my own production, New Theatre, 1934. This production ran for 155 performances, beating all the records for a *Hamlet* run since Henry Irving. Below: The Play scene: Laura Cowie (Gertrude), Frank Vosper (Claudius), Jessica Tandy (Ophelia), Jack Hawkins (Horatio), myself (Hamlet), and George Devine (First Player)

an all-American cast except for Malcolm Keen, who played the King, and Harry Andrews, who played Horatio. Rehearsals were thrilling because everyone seemed so excited about my performance. It was fearfully hot weather. We rehearsed on a roof somewhere and poured with sweat. I gave my all at those rehearsals, so anxious was I to impress the company.

At the time I was asked to go to America, I heard that Leslie Howard was proposing to play Hamlet there as well.[4] I said in that case I would not go. He was a great star and an Englishman and it would have been impertinent to put myself in competition against him. I signed my contract on the strict understanding that Howard would not do his production—and then, months later, he announced he would do it after all. He had an English cast, with Pamela Stanley and Clifford Evans and Lady Forbes-Robertson, the widow of the great Sir Johnston. Howard started on tour and the production I was in was the first to open in New York. My notices were interesting and reasonably kind, but though the reception on the first night had been overwhelmingly appreciative, I was doubtful of success. I remember cabling home and saying I thought we might run for six weeks with luck. Soon afterwards Howard's production opened and was not at all liked. The next day we had standing room only. It must have been a fearful blow to him and he naturally resented it very much and made speeches defending his performance. The gossip columns were full of it—it was called the 'battle of the Hamlets'—and the taxi drivers used to say to me, 'Which Hamlet are *you*?' The publicity people tried to get me to meet Howard and we were urged to go to see each other's performances, which we both refused to do.

It was slightly uncanny how our careers seemed to run on parallel lines. I met Howard only twice, and then merely for a chat and a drink, but I understudied him in a revival of *Berkeley Square* in which it was arranged that I should play some performances for him. I remember rehearsing the part but I never saw him in the theatre and I never went on. Later I was asked to play his part in *The Petrified Forest* in London and refused because I did not care for the play. Howard, of course, had made a huge success of it in America.

At the beginning of the Second War, Howard was in England. He did not go back to his home in Hollywood, he sold his polo ponies and went off to Portugal to give pro-Allies lectures. At about the same time—Christmas 1942—I went with a concert-party company, including Edith Evans and Beatrice Lillie, to Gibraltar. We went by plane and were told that there was no danger as we should be flying through a neutral zone. A few weeks later Leslie Howard was shot down and killed—in the very same plane. A little later, when I was playing at the Haymarket, I was sent the script of a film with a note from the producers saying that Howard was to have made the film and they could think of no better substitute than me. I was horrified, flung the script across the room and would have nothing to do with it.

My New York *Hamlet* broke the Broadway record for continuous performances previously set by Barrymore—101 performances. In fact, my record held until Richard Burton broke it in the mid 1960s, in a production directed by me, which seemed a little ironic.[5]

Hamlet is not, however, a role that an actor should ever be asked to portray for a hundred performances on end. There is such a range of opportunity in the part that it encourages you to try all sorts of different tricks and effects. You need a very strict director to keep you in line. When I directed Burton in *Hamlet* he told me that the one thing in which I had been able to help him was knowing where the rests were, so that he did not play too long on hysteria and nerves. I tried to make him find a real line for the part. The play is so familiar that the temptation is to play up the 'show' scenes—the closet scene, the nunnery scene, the play scene, the graveyard scene—instead of making it a play with progressions in which the audience does not know what is going to happen next. It was for this reason that I loved acting Hamlet to the troops during the war. Quite unfamiliar with the story, they followed it with breathless interest, wondering what would happen next.

I have had my fill of *Hamlet* now. So many books are written about the character but I cannot read them any more. Nor, I think, could I direct the play again. When I attempted to direct Burton I found it impossible to do anything new or interesting. I was surrounded by ghosts, not just that of Hamlet's father, but of all the other productions I had seen, acted in and directed. Burton was unhappy in Elizabethan clothes and so I thought of modern dress, of staging the play as if it were a rehearsal. I conceived a very interesting set, modelled on Craig's description of the Lyceum at rehearsal time, a tree from *The Bells*, a tombstone used in *Eugene Aram*, a great sledge and a gabled housefront from *Faust*, all huddled at the sides of the empty stage. I discovered, however, that an American audience would not understand such a set, as their theatres are stripped

completely after every production and need new scenery and lighting installed for every play. So I decided the cast should wear perfectly ordinary street clothes and play as if it were a rehearsal, using a walking-stick or umbrella as a sword, an overcoat to represent a cape and so on. They all spent fortunes on buying new clothes, but none of them seemed right. The King brought different costumes to rehearsal — panama hats, blazers, slacks, and the Queen brought a mink coat which did not look right either. The set, although it was rather impressive, was bare and bleak, and the audience had no idea what we were getting at. It was too theatrical an idea to succeed in the theatre! I played the Ghost myself. I recorded the speeches and projected a huge shadow on the stage — which I thought was the only really effective idea in the whole production.

The American cast did not appear to understand very much of what I was trying to do. All they wanted was motivation. Unfortunately, the Method does not work for Shakespeare. In 'intellectual' drama, Ibsen and Shaw for instance, a character's intentions are motivated very clearly, and his background too. There is a story of Barrie or Pinero saying at rehearsal 'Now remember, you have an aunt in Surbiton who wears grey felt bonnets.' In Shakespeare's plays, characters like Rosencrantz and Guildenstern, Salarino, and all those lords in the historical plays, are not developed individually, but can be turned into effective cameos if clever actors play them. In America I was attacked after every rehearsal by desperate actors asking 'What is this character *about*?' I fear that, in the end, my ill-tempered reply would be 'It's about being a good feed for Hamlet.' In England a young, ambitious actor takes these minor parts in his stride. He plays Oliver in *As You Like It* or Salarino in *The Merchant of Venice* or any of those supporting roles, and tries to find something to do with them, while waiting for the time when he will be allowed to play Orlando or Shylock.

The last time I ever played Hamlet was in the Cairo Opera House. It was a school matinée, packed with children, and as we started the play I thought 'Well, this is the last time I shall ever play this wonderful part. I'm forty-one and it's quite time to give it up.' Early on in the performance the unfortunate man who played Horatio fell into my arms in an epileptic fit on the line 'My Lord, I think I saw him yesternight'. The audience was bewildered as I shouted to the prompt corner, rather crossly, 'Drop the curtain. Put something between his teeth. Fetch the understudy.' The understudy came,

87

The New York *Hamlet*, 1936, with Judith Anderson as Gertrude.
'I felt I was on my mettle'

Left: *Hamlet* at the Lyceum, 1939, the last stage performance in Irving's famous theatre

Right: *Hamlet* at Elsinore Castle, 1939, with Fay Compton (Ophelia) and George Howe (Polonius)

Below: My last *Hamlet*, with Leslie Banks and Marian Spencer as the King and Queen, at the Haymarket, 1944 rescued from the bowels of the theatre where he was making up for Guildenstern, and did not know a line. When he pointed to the Ghost and said, 'Look my Lord it comes,' I said, 'No, you fool, the other way!' or words to that effect. Fortunately, the epileptic Horatio recovered the next day, but I could never quite forgive him for ruining my final performance of Hamlet!

Miss Baylis asked me to return to the Vic for the 1930 season at £20 a week. I was much impressed, knowing what an agony it was for her to increase a salary. Between the two Vic seasons Playfair asked me to go to the Lyric, Hammersmith, and play John Worthing in *The Importance of Being Earnest* with my aunt Mabel Terry-Lewis as Lady Bracknell, Anthony Ireland as Algy and Jean Cadell as Miss Prism. The production was entirely in black and white in the manner of Beardsley drawings and was a great success. It could have run longer if I had not had to go back to the Vic. We played it all through that very hot summer. One day, at a matinée, we were trying to play the muffins scene when I glanced at the audience and saw about six old ladies in different parts of the stalls all hanging over their seats fast asleep. I became quite hysterical and Tony Ireland and I were nearly sacked because we giggled so disgracefully.

In my second season at the Vic we were joined by Ralph Richardson.[6] I had seen Ralph quite often on the stage before I got to know him and work with him for the first time. He had been in a number of productions for Barry Jackson and was a friend of Frank Vosper, who was also a friend of mine.

Ralph is a remarkable man, shrewd, observant, warm and generous-hearted, once you get to know him. He is also reserved and cautious, never making a swift decision about anything. He did, however, make a very swift decision about me at our first meeting. He thought that I was affected and conceited and wore unsuitably dandy clothes. Gradually, however, we found we had a lot of interests in common, and one day when we were rehearsing *The Tempest* — he was playing Caliban and I was playing Prospero — he suddenly decided that I knew what I was talking about and that he liked my acting, and we have been the most devoted friends ever since.

We were both in *Henry IV Part I* with which the 1930 season opened. Ralph hated the fighting and I did not like it much either.

Right: Ralph Richardson and Edith Evans as Iago and Emilia in *Othello*, Old Vic, 1932

Below: The Black-and-White production of *The Importance of Being Earnest* at the Lyric, Hammersmith, 1930, with Mabel Terry-Lewis as Lady Bracknell. 'When she played Lady Bracknell with me she played it beautifully, but she had no idea why it was funny at all; she said "Why are they laughing? This line isn't funny to me"'

During the battle of Shrewsbury Ralph used to shout 'Left . . . right . . . now you hit me, Cocky . . . now I hit you' — I was sure the audience could hear him. He was not particularly happy as Prince Hal, but absolutely superb as Caliban and, later in the same season, as Enobarbus and Kent. In fact, I cannot imagine anybody playing them so well. He always took great pains with his make-up, for which he would make elaborate drawings beforehand. He and Olivier vied with each other in the construction of putty noses. I have always implored him to revive his Falstaff which he played in 1945 at the New Theatre, and which was, to my mind, a definitive performance. What a magnificent Peer Gynt he was in the same season, and how unforgettably good in Priestley's *Johnson over Jordan* and *Eden End*, and, of course, in so many successes since!

Ralph and I have always got on extremely well whenever I have acted with him or directed him. He knows that out of twelve suggestions I make two will be some good and the rest can be thrown in the dustbin. We are neither of us wildly intellectual but Ralph has a far wider range of interests than I do. He follows history and politics, he reads voraciously. He knows about clocks and furniture and china and motor cars and all things mechanical. He has endless hobbies. He is far less frivolous, theatrically, than I am. I have always adored the 'cheap' side of the theatre, the billing, the advertisements, the queues, the fan-letters and the somewhat unbalanced adulation of certain people whose admiration is extravagant and often insincere. Ralph, like Edith Evans, has enormous dignity and reserve where the public is concerned. Both were far more exercised about the quality of a performance than its effect upon an audience, whereas I am inclined to think to myself 'A jolly good house today, went marvellously and I made a lot of stunning effects, must try to remember to put them in again tomorrow night.' That was not the way of Ralph and Edith, both of them selective and economical in their work. (Oddly enough, when they played together, there was no great rapport — Ralph admired Edith, but I suspect that she found him too eccentric). Realistic actors, like Ralph, labour to find the core of a character. Until they have had time to study a role they do not want to be looked at or even criticized. By contrast, I am rather conceitedly ready to jump in and take a wild dash at a part at the first rehearsals. I find it difficult to work by myself at home. I develop a part during rehearsals with the company, make mad suggestions, throw them out and try some more. I am feather-headed and not

92

Macbeth, Old Vic, 1930: 'I knew I would not be able to play the warrior, but I found a romantic and visionary quality in the character'

really thorough. Now and again my method appears to work—so long as my fellow players are prepared to put up with it.

During those two seasons at the Old Vic I learnt a great deal about playing Shakespeare. What was so valuable was the opportunity of getting to know how to act with breadth for an enthusiastic, largely unlettered audience who did not resent us making broad effects. The fact that we worked for such small salaries, which placed restrictions on our social life in our salad days, was very good for us. It was exciting to find that I could do something with a part like Benedick. I was certainly not ideally cast for the role of a bluff soldier, and so I tried to find another way of playing it, as a kind of courtier. It was good experience and led to a good many similar experiments. I even played Antony in *Antony and Cleopatra*, for which I was utterly unsuited, but I padded my doublet and wore a false beard and shouted and boomed, and achieved some sort of result. I remember thinking that I could not learn the words because there were whole speeches I did not understand and there was no time to discuss or analyze them. So I tried a different approach, looking carefully at the punctuation and hoping the sense would in some way emerge. And I found that it seemed to help. Later, in *The Winter's Tale* and *Measure For Measure*, I began to trust to the sweep of a whole speech, concentrating on the commas, full-stops and semi-colons. If I kept to them and breathed with them, like an inexperienced swimmer, the verse seemed to hold me up and even disclose its meaning.

In *Macbeth* it was the imaginative side of the character that appealed to me. I knew I would not be able to play the warrior, the giant who cleaves people 'from the nave to the chaps', but I found a romantic and visionary quality in the character, and a weakness which emerges when his wife urges him to murder Duncan. My interpretation was the absolute opposite of Olivier's which was, to my mind, the definitive Macbeth. Olivier had murder in his heart from the moment he came on the stage.

I thought that Macbeth, when he first comes on, should be what everyone has said he is in the first two scenes, the great warrior chieftain, loyal to Duncan, victorious in battle, flushed with success. Then he meets the witches and afterwards comes home to his wife, and these two meetings, at such a critical moment in his career, suddenly topple him from his nobility. What is so wonderful about Shakespeare is that you can play the parts in many different ways. Olivier convinced me absolutely in his production and so did Ian McKellen in Trevor Nunn's Royal Shakespeare production at the Warehouse in 1977. It is the same with Lear. I tried to play Lear as a very great king who is destroyed. Olivier played him as an eccentric, half-mad before the play begins. All sorts of people have taken different views of the part, as of all the great Shakespearean roles, and if you play them up to the hilt you can be as interesting in one way as you can in another. That is what has given them such enormous appeal for actors over the years.

CHAPTER
FOUR

1931–1938

The years 1929 and 1930 had been exciting times for me. I was twenty-six, just the age when a young actor begins to feel his wings are sprouting. But I was also beginning to long to try my hand at directing, and during the thirties I began to fulfil this ambition. My desire to direct was in a large measure due to the Russian director Theodore Komisarjevsky.[1]

Komisarjevsky was a fascinating character, who looked like a little monk, completely bald and with the most enchanting smile. He had an impish, rather wicked humour, but was prone to 'Russian moods' when things were not going well, when he would maintain a grim silence. He loved young people, especially if he thought they had talent.

In 1925 I had been playing in one of the first performances in England of Chekhov's *The Seagull* at the Little Theatre. I played the young hero Konstantin and, in my black blouse and Russian boots, I thought I was very romantic and noble, though I was somewhat put out when the audience laughed loudly as I entered, a gun in one hand and an obviously stuffed bird in the other. Komisarjevsky came to see the production and made great fun of it, saying it was quite ridiculous and completely un-Russian. He had not long settled in England after early years working in Russia, France, Italy and New York. He was a friend of J. B. Fagan for whom he had designed costumes for his season at the Court, as well as directing one or two

97

Joseph Surface in *The School for Scandal*, Queen's 1937. 'My greatest personal acting success of the four plays in the Queen's theatre season'

Stage Society special productions. Although he thought our production was awful, he engaged me to appear for him in a season at a curious little theatre that had once been a cinema, over Barnes Bridge opposite Ranelagh—in those days a club for tennis, polo and theatrical garden parties. The impresario was a man called Philip Ridgeway, a big, coarse Philistine from somewhere in the north of England who had somehow conceived the idea of giving Komisarjevsky an opportunity to direct in some Russian plays at Barnes. Ridgeway had recently launched there a successful adaptation of Hardy's *Tess of the D'Urbervilles* which he was about to transfer—with Gwen Ffrangcon-Davies and Ion Swinley — to the West End.

Komisarjevsky collected an extremely interesting company and we opened in *Three Sisters,* which had not been seen in England before. It was a beautiful production, very simply done and with a number of very good actors in it. I played the Baron Tusenbach. I was somewhat bewildered because, in the text, it stated that I was a very ugly man and that this was why Irina, the third sister, refused to marry me; but Komisarjevsky said, 'Oh, that is all nonsense! You must play it as a juvenile—side-burns and a handsome uniform. The English public must have a romantic hero.' Naturally I thought this must be the correct interpretation, but I was somewhat dismayed by the fact his approach went completely against the implications of the author. He cut out all the references to the Baron being ugly. When I presented the play, years later, under my own management in 1938, with Michel St-Denis directing, Michael Redgrave played the Baron as a spotty, gangling young booby in steel spectacles. When he said goodbye to Irina in the last act and went off to be killed in the duel, the audience was touched because he was such a silly, vague character who giggled and played the piano and whom nobody took seriously.

Back in 1926 I was, of course, a very intense young actor and Komisarjevsky exploited my intensity, knowing, I suppose, that the British public was not sufficiently familiar with the text to notice what cuts and changes he had made. But the production, romantic as it may have been, was the beginning of a great success for him at Barnes.

Each member of the company was paid £10 a week and we all dressed in one room together. We played twice daily, as far as I can remember, and smart people came from the West End in their cars to see us. We became quite the fashion. After the *Three Sisters* run of five or six weeks, Komis asked me to appear in a play called *Katerina* by Leonid Andreyev (who also wrote *The Seven Who Were Hanged*). *Katerina* was a melodrama in which I was cast as the husband, a man of about fifty. Jealous of his wife and suspecting her of adultery, he discovers that she has a lover. His reaction to this as the play proceeds, is one of bewildered complacency. In the last act the wife is in an artist's studio, dancing almost naked, and then drives off in a sleigh with the artist who is giving the party, while her husband is left sitting despairingly in a corner meekly accepting a cigarette from her first lover, the object of his suspicions in the first act. It was an interesting part, but again I was over-intense in my performance. James Agate wrote, 'Mr Gielgud is becoming one of our most admirable actors . . . Twice in this play he has to make an entry upstairs from below stage. The first time is an occasion of great solemnity, but on the second he is merely paying a friendly call to do which it is unnecessary to put on the manner of one rising from the grave.' Mrs Patrick Campbell came to see the play and said characteristically 'You are very good and you ought always to wear a goatee!'

Ernest Milton played the artist and Jean Forbes-Robertson—that lovely, ill-starred actress—was also in the cast. It was a reasonable success though there were emergencies and difficulties through lack of money. On the first night of *Katerina* the production was not nearly ready and a very long-suffering pianist exhausted her entire repertoire of Chopin pieces while Komis and the stage manager, almost fainting with exhaustion, tried to change and set up the scenery. Komis' sets, both for the Chekhov and for *Katerina,* were wonderfully inventive and he lit them beautifully. He really was a man of remarkable all-round talents. He knew about lighting, architecture, scenery, and had a wonderful sense of grouping and movement. But he was also extremely perverse and unpredictable. Money did not seem to interest him very much, however, and he often agreed to work quite cheaply.

Later on, when I became more successful, I was always suggesting that Komis should direct me in West End plays because I admired his work so much. When I played Trigorin in *The Seagull* in 1936 I asked Bronson Albery, to whom I was then under contract, to engage Komis to direct the play, and he agreed. Peggy Ashcroft was Nina, Stephen Haggard Constantin, and Alec Guinness had the tiny part of a workman in the first act. Komis immediately designed a beautiful scene for the first act and boasted to me that the trees were all made of real silk and that the set would cost at least £1,000, an enormous sum in those days. 'Of course,' he remarked, 'Albery is just a tradesman!' At the first reading of the play he delivered a long harangue about how dreadful the English theatre was, with wretched actors, completely lacking in style. Edith Evans, who was to play Arkadina (and was marvellous in the part), sat listening and looking very cross indeed, and I feared she would never get on with him at all. We started rehearsing. Then, in the middle of the first act, when Arkadina stops speaking to listen to the voices of a choir singing on the other side of the lake, Komis said his favourite word, 'powse' (pause), Edith 'powsed'. She 'powsed' for five minutes, the longest 'powse' I have ever heard, and from that moment she and Komis were delighted with each other.

The Shakespearean productions which he afterwards directed were *avant-garde* to say the least, though the three he did at Stratford were highly successful, probably because they were largely improvized, with no more than six or seven rehearsals for each play. He did a fine *Lear* with the OUDS at Oxford and afterwards at Stratford with Randle Ayrton. But I did not care for his *Macbeth* at all though there were some thrilling moments in it. The costumes were almost modern dress. The opening scene, dominated by a rusty First War cannon on the stage, was like a deserted battlefield, and the witches crawled about searching for debris. This was most effective, but Fabia Drake, who played Lady Macbeth, wore an unfortunate head-dress that looked as if it was made of iron curl-papers. In *The Merchant of Venice* Komis made great use of the trap-door which had just been installed in the new Memorial Theatre stage. Belmont rose as a little tower through the floor, with Portia and Nerissa sitting on chairs on the roof, to play their first scene. In the trial scene he had a backcloth, like a Longhi picture, with wigged judges, depicted as sheep, painted on it. The actors' heads stuck out through holes. Portia wore spectacles — and a beard.

Some years later, in London, Komis made a disastrous attempt to direct *Antony and Cleopatra* with Eugenie Leontovich, who had recently made a great success as a Russian emigré princess in a play called *Tovarich* and did not speak good English. Donald Wolfit was Antony and Leon Quartermaine, as Enobarbus, was quite miscast. Everybody imitated the way Miss Leontovich said 'O weederdee degarlano devar' ('O wither'd is the garland of the war'), as *The Times* critic quoted it. It was the joke of the year. She wore a helmet with Georgian plumes and a dress with a long slit train revealing her bare legs. Komis changed the order of the scenes, opening the play with the soothsayer and Cleopatra's maids. It was a dead failure and ran only three or four days. But Komis thought it was a splendid joke.

In 1931 he did a really beautiful production for me of a play called *Musical Chairs* at the Criterion Theatre by a young and very talented writer called Ronald MacKenzie who had been a friend of mine at prep school and was doomed to be tragically killed in a car crash just after his play had been running a year.

The last time I met Komis was when I asked him to direct *Crime and Punishment* for me in 1947 in New York, and he behaved in a very strange way. As usual he did not ask a big fee, but he was frightfully rude to any foreigner in the huge crowd who came to the auditions. It was terribly cold weather—a blizzard in fact—and almost a hundred hopefuls stood in a queue outside the theatre, many of them foreigners because, being a Russian play accents did not matter. Whenever a German or a Jew came on to read, Komis turned his back. You never knew when he would become difficult. I remember once, in another play he directed for me, there was an actress he thought was no good. One afternoon she failed to appear and the stage manager said 'Oh, Mr Komisarjevsky, I'm sorry Miss So-and-So couldn't come this afternoon, she has a fitting.' Komis took a photograph of her which was on a table, dashed it to the ground and stamped on it. Yet, in spite of his temperament, Komis contributed a great deal to the theatre in the years he worked in England and had many successes. The stage hands all liked him and worked hard to please him. One of them referred to him as 'Come and Seduce me', which amused him very much.

He had a very emotional love-life and was always changing part-ners. I met him once in the country at the house of Constance Spry, the well-known florist. Komis was very taken by a lady novelist who was also staying there. Constance Spry had just designed a lot of costume jewellery and the ladies went upstairs and decked them-selves out in some of the necklaces and bracelets and then we all went into dinner at a beautiful table made of alabaster and lit from underneath. It was a summer night. I had seen Komis earlier in the evening sitting under a tree looking rather like Puck and refusing to be drawn into the conversation. After dinner we went into the drawing-room and I played the piano. When I got up to go home and

101

Left: Theodore Komisarjevsky:
'He looked like a little monk,
completely bald and with the
most enchanting smile. He had
an impish, rather wicked humour,
but was prone to ''Russian
moods'' when things were not
going well, when he would
maintain a grim silence'

Below: *Noah*, New Theatre,
1935, directed by Michel
St-Denis. 'Noah was got up like a
Breton peasant'

looked round to say goodbye to everyone Komis was nowhere to be seen. Finally I found him sitting under the piano with the lady he fancied, telling her fortune in a pudding-basin filled with candle-grease.

Komis was always moving from one country to another, adopting the new one for a few years and then becoming disillusioned. Finally, he went off to America, married a new wife and started an acting school. He died there a few years later.

Another director I admired greatly in the thirties was the Frenchman, Michel St-Denis.[2] For me, St-Denis' influence was as important as, though very different from, that of Komis. In 1931 St-Denis and his Compagnie des Quinze were giving a season at the Ambassador's Theatre in London. They put on *Noé*, *Le Viol de Lucrèce* by the company's resident dramatist, André Obey, and other plays. Like many of my confrères in the theatre, I was enormously impressed with these remarkable productions and the small but brilliant team of actors who appeared in them. *Noé* was simply the story of Noah and the Ark, written and presented in an extremely endearing and stylized way with the animals portrayed by actors in beautifully modelled masks with the effects and sounds done by the company.

In New York, Pierre Fresnay, then a young man of about my own age, who was a great friend of St-Denis, played the part of Noah in English. When I read an account in an English newspaper of his success I suddenly thought how effective and interesting it might be for me to try to play the part in London—a challenging contrast too after the long run of Hamlet. I obtained a translation of the play which had been made for the New York production, but it was a very poor one, and was full of slang phrases like 'Hey, you floozies!' and other regrettable Americanisms. St-Denis agreed to direct the play, but he did not speak English very well as he had only been here for a short time. We found the translation very unwieldy, and I never felt that it achieved the charm of the original. In the end I achieved some personal success in it, although I was never at ease in the part until almost the end of the run, which was only about ten weeks. It was fearfully hot weather and I had enormous quantities of padding, a huge beard and very heavy clothes, so that I was in great discomfort. Physically it was a demanding part, involving a great deal of balancing on planks and climbing ladders, and miming too, which in those days English actors were very rarely asked to attempt.

Michel came to rehearsal every day with complete notes of every movement, every piece of business, every characterization. He was not used to English actors, or to working quickly—we rehearsed only three weeks—and the whole production was somewhat hastily put together. However, I found it a good exercise, and, as has so often happened in my career, I learned a great deal from it. We learn as much, if not more, from our failures as we do from our successes. I tried hard to discipline myself in the technical problems of the part, to make myself believe that, as Noah, I was a practical working man. The play opened with me hammering and measuring the Ark with a ruler, considering its construction with the eye of a carpenter, but I had no idea how to tackle this and Michel had to teach me every move. He demanded great discipline and order from his actors. Komisarjevsky, by contrast, never had notes but would appear to improvize, though I think he had everything very clearly in his head. He was sympathetic to an actor's struggles, mistakes and experiments while St-Denis was something of a martinet, with a very orderly French mind.

My own first West End success as a director came in 1933 with *Richard of Bordeaux*, a new historical play written by Gordon Daviot. Gordon Daviot was a pseudonym for a lady called Elizabeth Mackintosh who came from Inverness and had written several successful thrillers and novels under various names, including some under the name of Josephine Tey. I thought her script for *Richard of Bordeaux* charmingly written, with vivid characters drawn lightly and without pomposity. The dialogue was simple, colloquial, rather in the manner of Shaw's *Caesar and Cleopatra*—great kings and nobles behaving and talking like modern human beings. The part of Richard was written with a great sense of humour, and was a splendid opportunity—the young, impetuous, highly-strung boy growing into a disillusioned man, his wife dying of the plague, and his best friend betraying him. Shakespeare's Richard, although a wonderful part for an actor, has no humour and can be monotonously lyrical—Daviot's play was amusing and its pacifist angle had a great appeal at the time when it was produced.

'The Motleys'—three talented girls who had trained together at art school—were just beginning then as stage designers. They had a little flat off Kensington High Street, where I used to visit them after they brought me some drawings they had made of me playing various roles at the Old Vic. They devised the clothes and the scenery for *Bordeaux*, simple but elegant, in very pale colours, gold and buff and white. Their décor was exactly right and greatly helped the success of the production. After the first two experimental Sunday nights at the Arts Theatre, Bronson Albery suggested that *Bordeaux* should be put on for a regular run. At first I was reluctant— there were so many things that I had felt were wrong with the play. However, I wrote to Gordon Daviot with some suggestions for changes. A few weeks later she sent me some excellent re-writes, small but infinitely valuable; a new scene for Bolingbroke to strengthen his part towards the end of the play; new lines here and there to improve Gwen Ffrangcon-Davies' part, Anne of Bohemia. In fact the text was so greatly improved that I became enthusiastic about it, especially as, under Albery's management, we could now spread ourselves a little and stage the play more lavishly.

The first night, on 2 February 1933 at the New Theatre, did not seem to be particularly successful, but there was another important opening on the same evening. Then the first matinée was suddenly sold out and the play became a tremendous hit. In fact, I had the greatest 'fan' success of my whole career. Crowds mobbed me at the stage door and often followed me home to my flat nearby, ringing me up, clattering my letter-box and sending me presents. Some of this delighted me, of course. It became somewhat exhausting at times, but now it is a pleasant thing to remember.

Richard of Bordeaux was a big stepping-stone in my career. Gordon Daviot wrote as much in the dedication of the copy of the play she gave me. It was a very much more realistic play than the cloak-and-sword dramas in the days of my Uncle Fred and Matheson Lang, though it had plenty of melodrama and excitement as well as comedy. As a result of its success Albery gave me an extended contract. My first play under his management had been MacKenzie's *Musical Chairs*. I did *The Maitlands*, MacKenzie's last play before he was killed, but it was not a success. Komisarjevsky, for some reason, failed to produce the same magic that had made *Musical Chairs* succeed—and I was myself miscast. However, Albery offered to let me play and direct *Hamlet* in 1934. In 1935 *Romeo and Juliet* followed this production, and then *The Seagull*. The result was that in the many plays that I worked in under the Albery management between 1931 and 1936, I had a wealth of fine opportunities.

After *Bordeaux* I did a lot of directing, my own productions of *Hamlet* and *Romeo and Juliet* as well as plays in which I did not act

Above: Mercutio (right) in my own production of *Romeo and Juliet*, with Edith
Evans (Nurse) and Laurence Olivier (Romeo), 1935

    Mercutio: The bawdy hand of the dial is now upon the prick of noon
    Nurse: Out upon you! what a man are you!
    Romeo: One gentlewoman, that god hath made himself to mar

Right: Laurence Olivier (Romeo), Glen Byam Shaw (Benvolio), myself
(Mercutio) and Geoffrey Toone (Tybalt) in the 1935 *Romeo and Juliet*

myself – Rodney Ackland's *Strange Orchestra*, Emlyn Williams' *Spring 1600,* Somerset Maugham's *Sheppey* and Ackland's adaptation of Hugh Walpole's *The Old Ladies*. I greatly enjoyed working with the actors and designers and trying to do justice to the staging of these plays, though I did not presume to interpret them with any marked originality. I merely tried to comply with the demands of the playwright concerned.

The completely original director can hardly be said to exist. Most of his ideas have their origin in memories and impressions of other plays and in experiences in his own life. It is indeed hard to define what 'directing' really is, beyond creating a good atmosphere at rehearsals and knowing, technically, how the actors should be disposed so that the right person is in the proper position at each important moment. Some of our best English actors used to be admirable directors and many of the old actor-managers always directed their own plays. Then came the fashion for non-acting directors like Komisarjevsky, Peter Hall and Peter Brook. (St-Denis had been an actor, but gave it up, the other three had not.) Actors are often more comfortable with directors who have been actors themselves because they understand the technical problems, but the danger for an actor-director is that he is tempted to impose his own acting style on the cast. An outside director, on the other hand, tends to bring out the individuality of each performer and creates a contrast of personalities rather than an all-over style. The all-over style can, however, if successful, produce an unforgettable effect. Brecht's company, the Berliner Ensemble, for instance, with *Drums and Trumpets, The Caucasian Chalk Circle* and *Mother Courage* at the Palace in 1956, impressed audiences with an individual style of playing, broad, defiant, rhetorical, which Brecht had evidently imposed on them.

Any company which has been together a long time creates a recognizable style, like the Compagnie des Quinze, or, in the contemporary theatre, the National and the Royal Shakespeare companies. On the other hand, I have always thought that however good repertory companies are they should be broken up from time to time. My own good fortune has been that, over the years, I have worked with such wonderful companies, afterwards parting from them on excellent terms, and then, a few years later, have come to work with them again. Acting with great artists like Edith Evans or Peggy Ashcroft, Laurence Olivier, Ralph Richardson or Alec Guinness, I find myself so much at home with them on the very first day of rehearsal that I can start work much more quickly than if I have to break the ice with players I do not know at all.

I have had semi-permanent companies several times over the years, once in 1937, once in 1944 and again in 1953. In *Richard of Bordeaux*, in my first years as a director, I was lucky enough to have three or four elderly actors who had been with Tree, Benson, Fagan and Playfair, yet they obeyed me without question and had beautiful manners. At the Haymarket at the end of the war, when I had a very senior company (although, as I discovered afterwards, two or three of them were not very fond of each other) their discipline and good behaviour was unfailing.

In the thirties when Olivier, Peggy Ashcroft and I were just beginning to make our first successes we often found that we would form a solid centre in a company, with two sides round us, one a group of very enthusiastic young people, like Anthony Quayle, Glen Byam Shaw, Alec Guinness, Harry Andrews, actors who were just beginning: and another, made up of highly experienced people like Leon Quartermaine, Cecil Trouncer and Leslie Banks. The young people matched with their youthful enthusiasm what the older ones had in experience—an ideal situation, it seems to me.

I first saw Peggy Ashcroft as Desdemona in the Paul Robeson *Othello* at the Savoy Theatre in 1930.[3] Ralph Richardson was Roderigo, Sybil Thorndike played Emilia and an actor called Maurice Browne played Iago and co-directed the production. It was a great failure. Robeson, who should have been superb, was not helped by an Elizabethan costume of padded trunks, square shoes and a ruff. It was not until the last scene, when he came on in a white kaftan, that he looked really magnificent. He had a fine singing voice, uniquely gentle and deep, but somehow not suited to blank verse. The scenery was by James Pryde, a very successful painter and a friend of Sickert, Craig and Nicholson in the 1890s. Together they had designed posters for Irving, under the name of the Beggarstaff Brothers, and did a famous one of him as Don Quixote, which I believe was never used. Pryde's scenery was rather impressive, like his pictures: unnaturally high shadowy rooms, a huge bed for Desdemona—but the sets were built too far upstage and they were dimly lit. It was

Sybil Thorndike as Emilia and Peggy Ashcroft as Desdemona in the Paul Robeson *Othello*, Savoy, 1930

Vershinin in *Three Sisters* (below right) directed by Michel St-Denis, Queen's, 1938, with (below) Leon Quartermaine (Kuligin) and Carol Goodner (Masha), in a cartoon by Hewitt

Right: *The School for Scandal*, directed by Tyrone Guthrie, Queen's, 1937. The scene of reconciliation between Sir Peter and Lady Teazle. Anti-clockwise, from top: John Gielgud, Michael Redgrave, Rachel Kempson, Leon Quartermaine, Peggy Ashcroft, Frederick Lloyd and Harcourt Williams

Marie Tempest in *Dear Octopus*, Queen's, 1938, directed by Glen Byam Shaw.
'An enormously skilled little lady with superb technical accomplishments'

impossible to see what was going on and there was a terrible noise from the scene shifters during the changes. But when Peggy Ashcroft first came on, in her gold dress, in the Senate scene, the audience sat up in their seats. It was as if the sun had come out. In the handkerchief scene she acted so lightly and so touchingly that her performance saved the evening. Soon after that I met her and asked her to play Juliet for me at Oxford with the undergraduates. She already had several London successes to her credit, so that when she and Edith Evans both agreed to come it was splendid for me as well as for the undergraduates.

I have directed Peggy so many times since – in *The Heiress*, the Goetz adaptation of Henry James' *Washington Square*, and Enid Bagnold's *The Chalk Garden*. She was my leading lady at the Queen's Theatre in 1937 and 1938, playing Portia, Irina, Lady Teazle and the Queen in *Richard II*. We were at Stratford together one whole season in 1950 and toured on the continent together in 1955. Unfortunately I have not worked with her for some years now. I have always loved her acting. She is the most perfect partner and her influence in a company is extraordinary. She helped Peter Hall tremendously during his years at Stratford and gave some wonderful performances for him, particularly in *The Wars of the Roses*, where she played Queen Margaret of Anjou right through from a young girl to an old hag, and her Hedda Gabler I thought was a *tour de force*.

I had done a season of four plays at the Queen's in 1937–38 and I was very tired when, out of the blue, Hugh Beaumont offered me a big salary to take part in a modern play, *Dear Octopus* by Dodie Smith, with Dame Marie Tempest. In those days, except for *Musical Chairs*, I never seemed to be cast in modern dress except to play prigs or bores – and my part in *Dear Octopus*, like that of Inigo in *The Good Companions*, made very few demands. However, I played those two parts in each case for nearly two years. Dodie's play had a very good cast with Angela Baddeley and Valerie Taylor, and Glen Byam Shaw to direct it, and it was fascinating to work with Marie Tempest.[4] She was an enormously skilled little lady with superb technical accomplishments, bright and intelligent in many ways, rather limited in others. I doubt if she had even read the piece when she agreed to appear in it but she trusted Beaumont's judgement implicitly and he was nearly always right. She was getting old and found great difficulty in learning her lines, but she was a rigid disciplinarian and worked like a demon all through rehearsals.

We went on tour for several weeks before opening in London, and Dame Marie would come down to lunch in the hotel dining-room in Newcastle wearing a beautiful hat and white gloves which she turned back at the wrist while she was eating. She would then retire to bed for the afternoon to rest. She did not get on very well with Dodie Smith and on the first night in London, when Dodie came on at the end to take a call with the company, Dame Marie turned her back on her in full view of the audience. To her great embarrassment, when she got home she found a six-page letter from Dodie, written after the dress rehearsal, thanking her and congratulating her and telling her what a genius she was.

The first night was memorable for another reason. It coincided with Munich. I remember at the party afterwards Noël Coward walked in with a grey face, saying that this was the most terrible thing that had ever happened, while we were all waving champagne glasses in honour of Mr Chamberlain's piece of paper. The play ran all through that very nerve-wracking year. It was a charming, cosy kind of a play and people loved it. The revival a few years ago with Cicely Courtneidge and Jack Hulbert was almost equally successful.

Marie Tempest played herself in every part. She adorned a number of forgotten little comedies at the small theatres that used to begin at 9 p.m. and end at 10.30 p.m., coming on in a series of smart frocks, snapping her fingers and twinkling as she made much play with a little lace handkerchief, and utterly bewitching the audience. Yvonne Arnaud had the same skill. Neither of the ladies could be said to be a great beauty, both were rather short and plump, but they had style. Dame Marie especially wore her beautiful clothes with a great air and knew just how far to go in dressing à la mode. She was always perfectly soignée, with beautiful shoes and crisp little hats.

The first time I ever saw Marie Tempest was in a revival of *Alice Sit-by-the-Fire*. But the part suited her no better than it had suited Ellen Terry for whom Barrie had written it originally. It was a thoroughly sentimental Edwardian piece. Later I saw her in an American farce about amateur theatricals, *The Torchbearers*, where she was extremely funny, and then she had a huge personal success in Coward's *Hay Fever*, in which she was inimitable. At her Jubilee performance at Drury Lane in 1937 she acted with the most extra-ordinary self-possession in three scenes from plays in which she had triumphed when she was young. At the end, dressed in a pink dress trimmed with ostrich feathers, she was carried on to the stage in a gold chair. All the stars of the London theatre were assembled in a huge group to do her homage, and her chair was put down in the middle of the stage. She curtsied to the Royal Box and made a charming little speech. Her calmness and control on such an emotional occasion was remarkable.

A number of other actresses celebrated in the Edwardian theatre were still active in the late twenties and thirties, notably the Vanbrugh sisters, Irene and Violet, Madge Titheradge and Lillah McCarthy who later became Lady Keeble.

The Vanbrugh sisters were remarkably alike in appearance.[5] Tall and imposing, beautifully spoken, they moved with grace, their feet encased in long pointed shoes. They were elegantly but never ostentatiously dressed, entering and leaving the stage with unerring authority, and always straight-backed when they sat on chairs and sofas. Violet never struck me as a natural comedienne, as Irene was, although she had appeared before my time in a number of comedies by Alfred Sutro and other contemporary authors. I remember her making a most effective entrance in a melodramatic play, *Evensong*, in which Edith Evans was sensationally good as a Prima Donna, a character obviously modelled on Melba.

Though Violet had achieved considerable success at His Majesty's with Tree, playing Lady Macbeth and Katharine of Aragon, I do not think either she or her sister could ever have been at their best in Shakespeare. Both actresses were very much of their own period. When I saw them, quite late on in their careers, playing *Merry Wives* in Regent's Park in 1937 for Sydney Carroll, they seemed to me very much like elegant Edwardian ladies romping about in fancy dress.

The sisters had both been sponsored in their girlhood by Irving and Ellen Terry. Their father was a clergyman, and such distinguished patronage may have been helpful in winning their parents consent to their going on the stage. Irene was an established star in the early twenties, when first I saw her in three light comedies by

A. A. Milne, and I was delighted by her brilliant performances in these pieces which, in her consummately professional hands, seemed much better than they really were. In Milne's *Belinda* she spent the first five minutes of the opening scene deciding how to swing herself into a hammock without showing too much leg (skirts were fairly short in this period) and I can see her now, amid the property hollyhocks and cut-out tree-wings, with Dennis Neilson-Terry as a languid poet in an impeccable grey flannel suit—how I longed to possess one like it—making love to her.

Her husband, Dion Boucicault, often acted with her, and usually directed her as well. A very small man (he was nick-named 'Dot') he looked delightfully absurd when he took a call with his tall wife at the end of a performance, especially on the huge stage of the Coliseum, where I once saw them in a one-act play of Barrie's called *Half-an-Hour*. Both Violet and Irene often appeared there in playlets which were given top billing in the variety programmes of the time.

Boucicault had the reputation of being a fine though somewhat daunting director and excelled, as Gerald du Maurier did afterwards, in teaching his women stars. Marie Tempest told me that, when she turned to straighter plays after her early successes in light opera and musical comedy, she owed her technique entirely to his teaching. He demanded meticulous pace and timing. Marie Tempest's personality was always crisp and twinkling with mischief, whereas Irene Vanbrugh was graver and more sedate, though equally brilliant in timing and expertise.

Both the Vanbrugh sisters retained their immense popularity to the very end of their careers and Irene's Jubilee, for which Noël Coward wrote a prologue, was a great occasion which I was sad to miss because I was in America. She had been acting just before this time in several small but delightful cameo parts—Lady Markby in *An Ideal Husband* and as the mother of the heroine in Coward's *Operette*. Fritzi Massary, the Viennese star, was also in the Coward piece, and these two veterans stole all the notices though they only appeared in one or two short scenes.

Irene had a very distinctive voice, extremely clear and ringing. In a very dull production of *The Swan* (adapted from Molnar and with a starry but uninspired cast) she appeared in the last act as the Queen Mother of some Ruritanian country. When her voice was suddenly heard behind the scenes just before her entrance the whole audience

The Vanbrugh sisters. Violet (right) and Irene (inset).
'Tall and imposing, beautifully spoken, they moved with grace'

began to sit up and take notice. And I can see her now in a revival of Maugham's comedy *Caroline*, delivering a long speech in a scene with her doctor as she lay on a sofa and suddenly capping it with a delicious upward inflexion as she looked slyly up at him and remarked 'You're *not* going to charge me a guinea for this, are you?'

Madge Titheradge, known to her friends as 'Midge', was small and appealing, eager and intense.[6] Her voice was somewhat hoarse but she knew how to adapt it with the utmost skill to the demands either of comedy or drama. Her dark eyes would brim with tears or shine with mischief. I have a recurring image of her in a brown dress with wide lace sleeves hanging loosely from her elbows, her arms flung out at some emotional moment in an attitude of crucifixion.

In the First War comedy *General Post* with Lilian Braithwaite, in which I saw her first, she was as delightfully romantic as she was in a ridiculous melodrama, *Tiger's Cub*, set in a log cabin with a baby in a shawl, Canadian Mounties and husky dogs barking behind the scenes. She was the long-suffering heroine of an adaptation of Robert Hichens' novel *The Garden of Allah* at Drury Lane, an impressive and soul-stirring spectacle featuring real camels and a real sandstorm. Unhappily on the first night the sand blew across the footlights, spraying the orchestra pit and the occupants of the first ten rows of the stalls.

She enchanted me during successive seasons in such different characters as the boulevard heroine of *Bluebeard's Eighth Wife* and as Nora in *A Doll's House*, in which she gave a thrilling performance, especially in the Tarantella scene. One Christmas, during the First War, she was Principal Boy in a Drury Lane pantomime, and recited (in armour I fancy) a patriotic poem of Alfred Noyes, 'A Song of England', holding the audience spellbound as she stood alone on the enormous stage.

On only two occasions did she disappoint me; as Desdemona to Godfrey Tearle's Othello and as Beatrice to Henry Ainley's Benedick. Evidently Shakespeare was the only author with whom she was not on easy terms, though before my time she had made a success as the French Princess Katharine to the Henry V of Lewis Waller, the famous Edwardian matinée idol.

In 1924, when Noël Coward achieved his first success with *The Vortex*, managements were eager to stage everything he had written. Madge Titheradge, whom Coward admired as much as I did, was announced as one of the two leading ladies in his *Fallen Angels*, but

118

she did not finally appear in the production. However, she acted in two of his later plays, *Home Chat* (a light comedy which failed to attract the public in spite of her amusing performance) and *The Queen Was in the Parlour*, a Ruritanian melodrama in which she was required to give up her throne in the cause of love—and very movingly she did it. Lady Tree, who also appeared in the play, must have shown her usual good nature in accepting the engagement, since rumour had it that she had been at one time a rival to Madge Titheradge in competing for Lewis Waller's favours. There was even a story that both actresses attended his funeral clad in widow's weeds, though the account was too discreet to mention what Mrs Waller's reaction may have been.

Madge Titheradge was very emotional both on and off the stage. She came to see *The Constant Nymph* one afternoon and fainted in the dressing room of Edna Best whom she had come to congratulate. Some years later she fainted (on the stage this time) as the curtain fell on the second act of *Theatre Royal* in which she was appearing. However, she recovered almost immediately on realizing that the redoubtable Marie Tempest was about to belabour her with the walking stick she used in the play. She was seldom seen in restaurants or in public, preferring, when she was not acting—which was very seldom—to stay at home and play bridge with her servants.

In 1928 I fulfilled a long-cherished ambition to meet and act with her when I was engaged to appear in New York for the first time. The play was an adaptation of a German costume drama about the murder of Paul I of Russia, played by the veteran actor Lyn Harding. I was the young Tsarevitch and Leslie Faber the principal conspirator, Count Pahlen, with Madge Titheradge as his mistress. I was sent for as a replacement, only arriving from England during the first dress rehearsal, and the play closed disastrously after a few performances. However, I had my first heady experience of speak-easy New York besides the privilege of acting, however briefly, with these three distinguished players. I found Madge Titheradge as fascinating and sympathetic as I had always felt sure she would be, and one evening she gave me a lift in her taxi and played a most affecting farewell scene for my private benefit, telling me she was resolved to leave the stage and marry a rich American. She kissed her hand as she waved goodbye and wished me well in the career that I was beginning, just as she was leaving hers forever.

Her future was sadly unlucky, as it turned out. Her husband lost

119

his fortune in the Wall Street crash and died not long afterwards and she was forced to return to the theatre after all.

On her return she was equally successful on the London stage for several years and I saw her give a splendid performance in *Promise*, a drama from the French of Henri Bernstein. Besides Edna Best and Ann Todd, the cast included Ralph Richardson, who was as greatly impressed by her artistry as I was.

She was equally effective in *Theatre Royal*, directed by Coward, with Marie Tempest and Laurence Olivier, and her last success was in *Mademoiselle*, another translation of a French play, also directed by Coward, in which she played a repressed governess with Isabel Jeans and Cecil Parker as two delightful comedy characters. But another play, which she had begun to rehearse, failed to come to London after some try-out weeks and she was never able to act again. Stricken with crippling arthritis, she lay bed-ridden for many years. I wrote to her once or twice but did not feel I knew her sufficiently well to ask her to let me go to see her. But I can never forget the pleasure she gave me in so many dazzling performances, and for me she will always epitomize a perfect example of professional expertise combined with unforgettable personal charm.

The first time I saw Lillah McCarthy on the stage she was appearing in a romantic melodrama called *The Wandering Jew* written by a popular novelist of the twenties, E. Temple Thurston, in which Matheson Lang, a fine actor of great power, played the leading part.[7] I had waited for many hours in a long queue to obtain a pit seat for the opening night and was sadly disappointed in the play, though I still remember much of it in some detail. In the opening scene, the procession to Calvary was supposed to pass an open window at the back of the stage, though only the top of the swaying cross was seen by the audience. Then the Jew returned, condemned to eternal reincarnation in different guises through the ages, having reviled Jesus behind the scenes.

The second act, which took place during the Middle Ages, was set in a pavilion (with a tournament supposed to be taking place off-stage) and Lang, in one of his various reincarnations, entered in chain-mail to become speedily involved with a handsome lady in a hectic seduction scene. As she struggled in his embrace, sinking onto a low couch with her back to the audience, her medieval robe was seen to be cut away revealing her in semi-naked splendour.

Why Lillah McCarthy should have bothered to appear in such a play baffled me considerably, for her taste was evidently far above the level of such tushery.

I must have seen her once before this however, in 1913, when she played Helena in the famous *A Midsummer Night's Dream* of Granville-Barker at the Savoy Theatre, but I was still a boy at the time and only have a dim recollection of the production: the gold-painted fairies, the swaying green curtains to suggest the wood, the hanging canopy overhead—a kind of chandelier of white and green —and the slim, tall figure of Oberon, my cousin Dennis Neilson-Terry. I recall also the slightly bewildered reactions of the audience whose older members remained nostalgically loyal to Mendelssohn, picture scenery and real rabbits, and a female Oberon who sang 'I know a bank' in a costume glittering with electric lights, in Tree's production at His Majesty's Theatre only a few seasons before.

Lillah McCarthy had been discovered by William Poel, who cast her as Lady Macbeth in one of his Elizabethan productions, patronized at that time by small but discriminating audiences, and Shaw was one of the first to spy out her talent at this performance. She later married Shaw's great friend and colleague Harley Granville-Barker and, working with them both, acted brilliantly in a wide range of parts in Greek Tragedy and many of the early Shaw plays during the first decade of this century.

She played the leading roles in *The Winter's Tale*, *A Midsummer Night's Dream* and *Twelfth Night*, and went to America to act in some of these productions at the beginning of the First War, but shortly afterwards her marriage to Granville-Barker broke up and she divorced him. Some years later she married again and was soon to leave the stage for good.

Her second husband, Professor Sir Frederick Keeble, lived at Oxford and they entertained their friends at a house on Boars Hill where Lady Keeble gave occasional poetry recitals to which aspiring undergraduates were often invited. She was also to be seen at first nights in London and at public dinners connected with Shakespeare and poetry. It was on one of these occasions that I met her first, introduced to her, I believe, by Elsie Fogerty, the famous voice coach who was such an invaluable help to so many young players—

121

Laurence Olivier, Peggy Ashcroft and myself. She was one of Lady Keeble's greatest friends.

I was, of course, impressed to meet such a famous actress though I found her somewhat awe-inspiring and difficult to talk to. But she was still beautiful and distinguished, though I did not dare to ask her questions about Granville-Barker, who had always been one of my greatest heroes, for I knew he had refused to allow either his name or his work to be mentioned in the autobiography she had recently written.

I did not meet her again for some years, until, after a matinée of Christopher Fry's *The Lady's Not for Burning*, in 1949, Lady Keeble came round to my dressing room and congratulated me. But she embarrassed me somewhat by asking that my leading lady, Pamela Brown, should be sent for in order to receive similar congratulations. I could not help thinking this to be rather autocratic behaviour on her part, though perhaps, as she was no longer young, she did not relish the prospect of climbing another flight of stairs.

A good many years later, as I was walking one winter day in Hyde Park, I noticed two elderly ladies, both looking extremely depressed by each other's company, seated on a bench near Rotten Row. Recognizing one of them as Lady Keeble, I thought it only proper to stop for a moment and pay my respects. She seemed delighted to be recognized, and, to my surprise, promptly invited me to come to tea with her at her flat in Gloucester Road on the following Sunday afternoon.

I ascended in a creaky lift to the top floor where the windows of her flat looked out on to a superb view of London, from the Empress Hall on one side to Big Ben and the Abbey on the other, a magnificent panorama of snow-covered roofs and towers.

My hostess greeted me with unexpected warmth and cordiality and offered me tea, followed by a large whisky and soda. Dressed in an extremely becoming Oriental-looking trouser suit, she poured a drink for herself, lit a cigarette and, tucking up her feet on a big divan covered with cushions, began to talk with the greatest freedom and enthusiasm. As before, I felt I should take care not to mention Granville-Barker's name, but to my great astonishment she started to tell me how she had first seen him at Cheltenham, when he was still a boy, dressed in a sailor suit and assisting his Italian mother in a recital, at which he spoke several of the poems himself.

She continued with fascinating reminiscences of their married

partnership and of the efforts made by Granville-Barker, with
Vedrenne and Bernard Shaw, to start a campaign to find money for
an English National Theatre. She told me of a weekend she once
spent at the country house of Sir Carl Meyer, a very rich man with a
hobby of growing prize carnations in his hot-houses. Granville-
Barker had urged her to accept the invitation (though he did not go
himself) in the hope of winning Meyer's financial help, and Sir
Herbert Tree, who had somehow got wind of the party, managed to
get himself invited too. As the guests prepared for their departure
on Monday morning, Sir Herbert (famous as an enthusiastic
ladies' man as well as a superb character-actor and impresario)
asked Lillah to share his first-class carriage back to London,
though he asked that she would not interrupt his concentration by
talking during the journey, as he had to study the script of a play
which he had promised to read.

'After a short time,' Lady Keeble told me gravely, 'he threw the
manuscript aside, left his seat by the window, crossed the carriage to
where I was sitting and attempted to fondle me. Of course, I managed to defend myself successfully, but, in the ensuing struggle, the
bouquet of carnations, presented to me by Sir Carl before I left,
became severely damaged and the flowers were strewn all over the
carriage floor by the time we arrived at Victoria Station. On leaving
the platform Sir Herbert bade me a polite farewell, waved me to a
cab, and hailed a separate one for himself, remarking that if we
should be seen arriving together at the stage door of his "beautiful"
theatre, eyebrows might justifiably be raised!'

Enchanted by these fascinating disclosures, I wrote an enthusiastic note of thanks as soon as I got home, only to receive next day a
letter in which Lady Keeble said she too had much enjoyed my visit
but feared our conversation had been rather too frivolous. She hoped
I would call on her another day to discuss the condition of the
modern theatre, about which she was seriously disturbed. But, alas,
only a few weeks later she was dead.

It must have been some time in 1928 that I met Ruth Draper for
the first time at one of Lady Colefax's lunch parties.[8] Sibyl Colefax
has been disparaged in recent memoirs, and even during her own
lifetime, as a snob and a lion-hunter. Nevertheless I was extremely
fond of her and grateful for the wonderful opportunity she gave to
young artists like myself to meet many literary, political and theatrical figures of the time whom we should never have had the good

fortune to encounter without her hospitable invitations. A few days after the party I went to see Miss Draper's unique one-woman show. She had, of course, been admired in London long before I first saw her—indeed I remember being intrigued as a very young man by the poster she used for the few public recitals she then gave, the famous charcoal sketch which John Sargent drew of her with a shawl draped over her head.

The curtained stage was empty save for a few pieces of essential furniture; a sofa, a couple of chairs and a table. Ruth Draper walked on, a tall, dark-eyed woman in a simple brown dress, beautifully cut, and looked out over the auditorium with grave composure. Her authority and concentration were absolute. How swiftly she transformed that stage into her own extraordinary world, transporting us to other places, other countries—a boudoir, a garden, a church, a customs shed; London, New York, Rome, the coast of Maine—creating in each of those imagined settings a single dominant character and then seeming to surround herself, as and when she needed them, with an attendant crowd of minor figures—children, animals, servants, husbands, lovers. Her wit and imagination could not fail to fascinate and never palled, however often I returned to see her famous monologues.

After the performance I went round to see her in her dressing-room and found her immensely sympathetic and delightful. The trenchant, acid wit which often sharpened many of her stage creations was not in the least evident in talking to her in private life.

I cherish in particular three occasions connected with Ruth. The first was an evening in New York when, at the end of a dinner party, she invited a small group of us back to her flat, and there, in front of the fire, as we all sat around in chairs or on the floor, she acted several of her sketches for us. It was a privilege to observe her at such close quarters and in such intimate surroundings.

The second was an afternoon in London. The great singer Kathleen Ferrier was dying of an incurable disease and some friends of hers, Ruth Draper among them, had taken a beautiful ground-floor flat looking out onto a very pretty garden so that she might recuperate after several weeks in hospital. I was invited to go to see her there and found Ruth standing beside her bed. We all tried to behave quite naturally, talking and laughing as best we could, with Miss Ferrier, radiantly beautiful, sitting up to greet us in a little pink jacket edged with white fur while she held Ruth's hand, and waving gallantly to us all as we bade her farewell.

On the third occasion, I had taken an American friend who had never seen her to one of Ruth Draper's last performances at the St James's Theatre in London, and when we went round to her dressing-room she was standing on a white drugget, looking much smaller than I remembered her, greatly aged and a little deaf. Yet only a few moments before I had watched her final sketch—a new one to me—in which she portrayed a temperamental Polish actress full of fire and emotion, speaking at a tremendous pace in an amazing mixture of languages.

During one of her last London seasons she made a few television versions of some of her sketches. These have never been shown, I believe, and I only hope they are somewhere in the archives, preserved for a generation that never had the privilege of seeing this consummate artist.

John Worthing in *The Importance of Being Earnest*, Globe, 1940.

CHAPTER
FIVE

1939–1945

In 1939 I went to Elsinore in Denmark to play Hamlet in the courtyard of Kronborg Castle, following the example of Laurence Olivier, who had inaugurated the Festival two years before. In that production, which Tyrone Guthrie directed, Vivien Leigh played Ophelia and Lilian Baylis was in attendance to provide sandwiches and encouragement, insisting that the courtyard clock should be stopped from striking because it interfered with the performances.

The outbreak of the War was only two months away when we arrived and we were instantly aware of the tension and mixed feelings everywhere. Besides this, our performances were marred by cold, rainy weather and we were not best pleased when, after some rather poor attendances, one night we saw a group of German sailors from a battleship occupying the whole of the front row of seats, even though they proved to be the quickest and most responsive members of the audience.

The trip did hold one treat for me, however: we were introduced to the mysterious and fascinating Baroness Blixen who took us all under her wing and made a moving and splendid speech in English about Shakespeare at one of the rather tedious lunch parties given in our honour by the Danes.[1]

It was difficult to tell her age. She had magnificent eyes, heavily made-up, and was rather small in stature, usually wearing black dresses and small hats with feathers and a veil. Her clothes were elegantly worn but simple, her manner friendly and welcoming in the extreme. I soon discovered that she was the famous Isaak Dinesen, author of *Out of Africa* and *Seven Gothic Tales*, though she never seemed to want to discuss her own work. We became friends immediately, and a year later, in 1940, she wrote to me saying she was coming to London where she hoped to find material for some articles she had been commissioned to write by the leading news-paper in Copenhagen, 'documents humains' dealing with all the European countries involved in the War. I arranged to give a party at my house in her honour, but during that very week Denmark was occupied by the Nazis, and she shut herself up in her family home at Rungsted to remain there for the rest of the war and write an anti-Nazi novel under an assumed name.

Karen Blixen had a genius for descriptive conversation. Hearing her talk, in her deep-voiced accent, was like listening to a fascinating short story, whether the subject happened to be Shakespeare, myth-ology, nights on the African veldt hunting lions, a visit of the Duke of Windsor to her farm in Kenya to see forbidden African dances, a radio appeal she had once made to ask for subscriptions to turn her orchard into a bird sanctuary, or the beauty of the sea sparkling below her house in Denmark, when the yachts were once more able to sail there and she knew the German occupation was over at last.

Ten years or so after the War, when I was in Paris to give a recital of my Shakespeare programme *Ages of Man*, I suddenly came face to face with Karen in the Rue St-Honoré. She was marching along flanked by two apple-cheeked Danish girls, who tactfully immolated themselves against the railings of the church which we were passing as she and I embraced each other in delighted recognition. I found she was staying in the same small hotel as I was, the 'France et Choiseul' (now much grander than it was in those days), with its charming square central courtyard and suites of rickety, plush-covered furniture. We ate ices together at a splendid confectioners, Latinville in the Rue St-Augustin, and that evening she came to hear my recital. We laughed and chatted happily together as if we had known each other all our lives. She was greatly changed in appear-ance, however, and when I went to Copenhagen to give my recital there some months later she was too ill to see me, only sending me her love and a huge bouquet of roses to my hotel.

But after a while she was a little stronger, and when I was playing in *The Tempest* at Stratford-on-Avon in the fifties she wrote telling me she was in London and greatly excited at the prospect of coming down to see a matinée. She adored the play but had never seen it performed, and one of the stories in her new collection *Anecdotes of Destiny* had been inspired by reading it. She came on to the stage at the end of the performance but was too frail to climb the stairs so I went down to talk to her and see her safely to her car. She wrote to me afterwards that her day had been perfection. Not only had she seen *The Tempest* and stood on Clopton Bridge to look at Shakespeare's river and the swans, but, on getting into the train at Leamington, she had been asked to mount guard over a number of dogs while their owners, who had been exhibiting them at a Birmingham Dog Show, left for the restaurant car to have their tea. This, she said, was a final delight for her at the end of her unforgettable experience at Stratford.

In 1959 I happened to be working in New York. I had been given an introduction to an elderly lady, a Mrs Murray Crane, and she had invited me to tea in her spacious and beautiful apartment on Fifth Avenue. The men at the party were mostly fairly young, several of them officials at the Metropolitan and the Museum of Modern Art, and the two most important lady guests were Karen Blixen and Edith Sitwell. I had first met Dame Edith at a luncheon at Sibyl Colefax's in London and had been charmed and surprised to find her so easy to talk to and so ready to make sly remarks about her own strange taste in clothes and jewelry. As a young man I had once been invited to a supper party in a studio near Bond Street and had met her two brothers, Osbert and Sacheverell, who also fascinated me with their brilliant conversational powers. How rare it is to sit at a table with really witty and generous hosts, who can shine spontaneously and rivet one's interest without making one feel totally inadequate oneself.

I discovered that, in New York, Karen Blixen was being fêted by everyone who knew her work. She was speaking in colleges and on the radio and appeared in a television interview. She looked frailer than ever, wearing a black hat like a coal scuttle which almost concealed her face, her body seemed shrunken and her wrists and ankles pitifully thin. But she was still able to hold her own with Edith Sitwell and the intellectual young men in Mrs Crane's apartment, amid the silver trays and cakestands, like a scene from a novel by Henry James.

I saw her once more after this, in 1962, not long before she died. I lunched with her at her charming house near Copenhagen with its porcelain stoves and long *broderie anglaise* curtains trailing on the polished floor. There she sat at the head of her table, surrounded by young people, tasting a few oysters and a glass of champagne, the only food and drink she was still able to swallow. Before I left she walked with me round her rambling garden, leaning heavily on my arm. 'That is where I want to be buried,' she said, pointing to a knoll at the top of the hill, 'but I mustn't tell the priest because my favourite dog is already buried there and I'm sure he wouldn't approve.' Then, as we turned the corner and saw the white sails of the yachts skimming over the water below, she spoke of the Nazis leaving and her unhappy time during the occupation. When I kissed her goodbye and drove away I knew I would never see her again.

The outbreak of the Second War naturally transformed everything in the theatre. I was extremely lucky not to be called up, the authorities taking the view that I could do a better job by staying in the theatre. I found myself living, somewhat precariously, from one production to another.

I remember that on the day war broke out I had started rehearsals for *Rebecca*, Daphne du Maurier's play, in which I was to star with Celia Johnson. Michel St-Denis was next door at the Queen's Theatre rehearsing *The Cherry Orchard*, with Edith Evans and Ronald Squire, and we all met in the pub during the lunch break. I had decided not to go on with *Rebecca* and I told them why: 'It's a commercial play, very good for peace-time, but I don't think it's the right thing to do now. Perhaps I can go back to the Old Vic for a bit and do something classical.' It was Guthrie, I think, who suggested that we should do *Lear*. He and Lewis Casson remembered that Harley Granville-Barker had written a fine preface to the play and thought he might be persuaded to help us. And so we wrote and asked him and he agreed.

Granville-Barker had become disillusioned with the theatre after the break-up of his first marriage to Lillah McCarthy. He had fallen madly in love with a rich American lady called Mrs Huntingdon who disliked the theatre and treated it as a kind of disagreeable mistress. Whenever Granville-Barker attempted to come back to the theatre she encouraged him to forget it and to live a pseudo-aristocratic life. For a time they had a large country house in England and attempted the roles of Lord and Lady of the Manor but it did not last long. In London they always stayed in a suite at the Ritz and Granville-Barker would never meet the press and only very few people in the theatre. He broke with Shaw altogether, though he remained devoted to Barrie. He lived in Paris during his last years, where he had a beautiful house and entertained all the eminent people, lecturing at the Sorbonne as well as working on his brilliant prefaces to Shakespeare. This was all very different from the young genius, eating nuts and wearing sandals, acting and directing in London, intensely violent and passionate about everything. He was to become one of my greatest heroes and the letters he wrote me over the years are among my treasured possessions.

When he first came to work with us on *Lear* in 1940, he had not been in the theatre as a director for many years. He did not know any of the younger actors and kept suggesting that Nicholas Hannen and Lewis Casson should play some of the young parts, not realizing that they were twenty or thirty years older than when they had all worked together as young men. But, of course, he was delighted to meet them again and when he began to work with younger people like myself he was able to sum us up in a very short time, knowing exactly which of us was worth taking trouble over.

I had worked with him once before, when we did *Hamlet* in 1939 at Elsinore. Before going to Denmark we had a try-out for a week at the Lyceum, which was about to be pulled down. This was in fact the last time it was used as a theatre. I heard that Barker was going to be in London and wrote to him. He agreed to come to a run-through on condition that 'there won't be any press or publicity — my name is not to be used in any way'. We acted the whole play for him and next morning he sent for me at the Ritz. I had the great distinction of keeping Mrs Granville-Barker out of the room for three hours —though she kept trying to get her husband away to go to a lunch. He sat on the sofa with a new edition of *Hamlet* in his hand, cutting the pages with a paper-knife as he went along and giving me notes at a great rate. I scribbled away with all my might, determined not to let him get away until he had finished. Then I rushed off and rang the theatre where the company was waiting and said 'I've had three hours with Granville-Barker, he has told me wonderful things about the production that can improve it. Would you be willing to rehearse again tomorrow [a Sunday] to try to put them in?' and they all agreed.

Working with Granville-Barker on *Lear* in 1940 was one of the

Above: Harley Granville-Barker as a young man, in 1905: 'He was to become one of my greatest heroes'

Right: *King Lear*, Old Vic, 1940, co-directed by Lewis Casson and Harley Granville-Barker, who once wrote to me:

My dear Gielgud. Did we ever agree as to the precise moment at which Lear goes off his head?

I believe that Poor Tom's appearance from the hovel marks it. The 'grumbling' inside, the Fool's scream of terror, the wild figure suddenly appearing — that combination would be enough to send him over the border-line. Do you mark the moment by doing something quite *new*? Difficult, I know, to find anything new to do at that moment, but something queer and significant of madness, followed (it would help) by a dead silence, before you say (again in a voice you have not used before)

'Didst thou give all . . .'

great experiences of my career. He came down every morning, his red eyebrows shooting out like Shaw's, wearing a bowler hat and a business suit, and we hung on his every word. He never praised you and he never tore you to pieces. He was quite impersonal, calling everybody by the name of their part or by their own surnames—none of the 'dears' and 'darlings' in which we are apt to indulge in the theatre. He was determined not to get caught up in any sort of publicity nonsense, interviews or photographs. He had laid down his terms clearly enough: 'I will come for those ten days for you only if nothing is said to the press.' Of course the news got out in the end and he left before the first dress rehearsal, which was terribly disappointing.

Tyrone Guthrie and Lewis Casson had been preparing the play for two weeks before he came, but when he arrived he changed everything they had done. He had previously come to London for one day to let me read over the part with him, and at the end of the reading he said to me 'Well, you've got two lines right. Of course, you are an ash and this part demands an oak, but we'll see what can be done,' which I thought was pretty shrewd. He knew exactly what he wanted to say and do. He would take infinite pains to achieve what he thought necessary yet was always prepared to give an actor a certain amount of latitude. He was no sergeant-major, forcing us to adopt his own tones and inflections; somehow he *implied* what he wanted. He was wonderfully perceptive musically; he knew just where the voice should rise, just where it should be sustained or dropped.

To me he was like a masseur who forces you to discover and use muscles you never knew you possessed. I remember rehearsing the last scene of *Lear* one night very late and he stopped me on every two words to give me inflections and tones. And I thought that at any moment he would say 'Now don't act any more, we'll work it out technically.' But he never did. So I thought I had better stick it out and keep going if I could with full emotion. By the time I looked at my watch we had been at it for forty-five minutes and I had never stopped weeping and ranting, but he found me a way to do the speech that night which I have never varied since.

Someone afterwards said that Granville-Barker spoiled my first entrance in *Lear* by ignoring the convention that the leading character should always come on from the centre. But in *Lear* the throne has to be in the centre for the opening scene. Irving got round the problem by coming down a great staircase at the side of the throne, but I've seen a drawing showing that he also sat at one side of the stage. Granville-Barker put the throne dead centre, with the six seats, for the other principal characters, placed three on each side of Lear, and the whole scene worked out in an absolutely symmetrical way. He declared that the much-held view that the first act of *Lear* is impossible, that Shakespeare wrote a ridiculous story, was nonsense. He told us to think of it as something from the Old Testament or one of the great fairy stories — 'Once upon a time there was an old king with three daughters' – and it illuminated it for us all.

I do not remember Granville-Barker saying much about the characters of Goneril — played in this production by Cathleen Nesbitt — and Regan — played by Fay Compton. He had worked with Cathleen Nesbitt years before, when she had played Perdita in his *The Winter's Tale*, but it was the first time that he had worked with Fay Compton. She realized at once what a fine director he was, and although so many of her successes had been in sentimental and sympathetic parts — in *Mary Rose* and *Quality Street*, for instance — in *Lear* she played Regan as a kind of cold pussy-cat, a wonderful conception. I remember Granville-Barker invented a tiny piece of business for her in her short scene with Oswald, after the blinding of Gloucester and the death of Cornwall. He had her making up her face, dressed in widow's weeds, with a mirror in her hand.

After rehearsal, Granville-Barker would say 'You did some very good things today, I hope you know what they were,' and would then produce a page of shattering, critical notes, which I wrote down at the time. I once asked him about the scene when Goneril is cursed by Lear and he leaves the stage on a very high note. A few lines later he returns in a totally different mood, in tears. 'What! fifty of my followers at a clap, Within a fortnight?' I asked Granville-Barker how Lear knows about the dismissal of his followers. Who told him? Granville-Barker replied that it does not matter. There is, he said, no off-stage time in Shakespeare: it did not come in until Ibsen, Pinero, Galsworthy and Shaw. In their plays you leave the stage to write a letter, stay off the stage for exactly the ten minutes it takes to write the letter and then come back. But Shakespeare knew how to convey an effect of time passing without realism. In this particular case the audience accepts the fact at once that somebody has told Lear the news offstage. In the same way Macbeth and Hamlet become older during the course of the plays, but we are not sure of their exact ages—whether Hamlet is very young, or thirty, as the grave-digger says—or of the actual lapse of time, though it is obvious in *Hamlet* that a considerable time passes during the action. In *Macbeth*, also, the last act is usually played as if months, or possibly a year or two, have passed. Shakespeare does it in a very simple way, knowing that the audience will not be aware of such exact details while they are watching, whereas critics, students and experts have spent years trying to work out the niceties of time—whether Cassio could actually have had time to seduce Desdemona, and so on.

For this privileged production we had a splendid cast—Fay Compton, Jessica Tandy, Cathleen Nesbitt, Robert Harris, Jack Hawkins, Stephen Haggard—and there was a tremendous feeling of urgency and excitement. It seemed to take our minds off the awful things that were happening in France. When people used to come round I would say 'How can you stand seeing so agonizing a play when such terrible things are going on in the world?' and they would answer that it gave them a kind of courage. It was a catharsis; you felt at the end of the play that the old man had learnt something from all the ghastly things that had happened to him, and the glory of the play and its magnificent poetry took you out of yourself. Shakespeare has always had that extraordinary appeal for every kind of audience. I felt it again when I played Prospero, and again when I played Hamlet abroad to the troops at the end of the War.

One of the earlier and most successful of my wartime productions was *The Importance of Being Earnest*, which we toured all over the country and then brought back to London, where we had first launched it for a few special matinées in 1939. After one of the performances Lord Alfred Douglas came round to see me, and soon after I met him again at a friend's house in the country. I had a cottage at Finchingfield in Essex in those days and one of my neighbours was A. J. A. Symons, who founded the Wine and Food Society and wrote a clever book on Frederick Rolfe, called *The Quest for Corvo*. At the time he was also trying to write a life of Wilde but was to die before he finished it. I went in one night and had drinks with Symons on the terrace of the house when Douglas was staying with him. They were a somewhat sinister pair and I was very disappointed in Douglas. Not only had he no longer a trace of his famous good looks but he was not very interesting to talk to either. He started on Wilde almost before I got through the door—Wilde was obviously his King Charles's head. I asked him a lot of pertinent questions about the original production of *The Importance of Being Earnest*, but all he could say was 'Oh, I stood at Oscar's shoulder all the time when he was writing the play at Worthing.' He could tell me nothing of the way in which it had been originally played; how much it was caricatured, all the nuances which I longed to discuss with him. Presumably he was not really interested in the theatre at all. I felt it must have been tragic for him to lose his beauty.

In 1942 I was asked to arrange a Christmas revue for the troops in Gibraltar. I commissioned various people to write sketches and collected a brilliant company which included Edith Evans, Beatrice Lillie, Michael Wilding, Elizabeth Welch and Phyllis Stanley. We were not quite sure what Edith Evans would want to do. Suddenly I remembered a benefit in which Edith and I had appeared at the beginning of the War. We had performed the great courtship scene between Mirabell and Millamant from Congreve's *The Way of the World*, one of Edith's most brilliant early successes. So I suggested that we should get somebody to write a little poem which Edith could recite in her Millamant dress, to open our revue. I commissioned a very nice woman, the wife of an actor, who composed satirical poems for the *New Statesman* under the name of Sagittarius. It was a very simple poem: 'We thought of you when to and fro/We wandered in the streets you know,/And as we acted in a play . . .' and so on. I showed it to Edith and she liked it very much. However, she thought there was one verse too many and in rehearsal cut the last verse. On the first night in the charming little theatre in Gibraltar the men were wild with excitement. They had seen no kind of live entertainment for two or three years and they knew there were some famous names on the bill. I went to the back of the auditorium to see the opening. The lights went up on Edith, dressed in her beautiful eighteenth-century Millamant costume, with beauty spots on her face and a white wig. To my horror, there was a most enormous laugh from the audience. I thought 'My God, they've never seen a woman dressed like this before and they think she's a Pantomime dame.' Edith stood her ground. She spoke her three verses perfectly—not the fourth, which she had been clever enough to cut—stood quite still for a moment and then swept off the stage. The house came down. She received a tremendous ovation. Her coolness and

John Worthing in my own production of *The Importance of Being Earnest*, Globe, 1939/40, with Gwen Ffrangcon-Davies as Gwendolen and Edith Evans as Lady Bracknell

Edith Evans in *Christmas Party Revue*, Gibraltar, 1942:
'Her coolness and authority completely conquered the audience'

authority had completely conquered the audience. It was very moving, and at subsequent performances they never laughed again.

The man responsible for all such entertainments for the troops during the War was, of course, Basil Dean, head of ENSA. Nobody thought he was particularly good at it and he was certainly fairly unpopular. I remember him once suggesting to me that I should take a play called *Diplomacy* to the troops. I had heard of this famous piece (a great standby of the Bancrofts and the Kendals and revived as late as 1934 by du Maurier with great success), but I had never seen it. So I took a copy into St James's Park and read it. I was absolutely dismayed. It was a wildly old-fashioned melodrama about a female spy, whose identity is betrayed by her scented gloves, and an innocent heroine who crucifies herself against a door. Four remarkably elaborate sets are needed, and the elaborate costumes of the 1880s. It would have been quite impossible to stage and I am sure the troops would have found it utterly ridiculous.

Dean had worked with a number of the best actors in his company before the First War at Liverpool. He had brought some of them to London backed by Alec Rea, a rich shipping magnate, and established himself in a series of productions at the newly-built St Martin's Theatre. After the First War, the men who came back, like Leslie Banks, were longing of course to start acting again and Dean was clever enough to collect fine companies round him. He still called himself Captain Basil Dean for long after the First War was over and went on behaving rather as if he was still a soldier, ordering everybody about. However, he chose good contemporary authors — Galsworthy, Masefield, Lonsdale — and had a sensitive feeling for poetry and spectacle and romantic theatre. James Elroy Flecker's *Hassan*, Dean's most cherished project, looked very handsome. The sets were by George Harris, his favourite designer and great friend.

When Harris died, Dean was shattered. This, and the death of Meggie Albanesi, a young actress whom he had discovered and who made an enormous success in several of his productions in the early 1920s, was a great grief to Dean and I doubt if he ever recovered afterwards. He certainly had a flair for casting and in rehearsal he was meticulous and extremely efficient. The only play in which I worked for him was Margaret Kennedy's *The Constant Nymph*, in which he was rather unkind to me, but I did appreciate how well he had arranged the play. I think he was too cold a personality to inspire actors to poetic work, good though he was for realistic stuff;

Basil Dean as Jack Barthwick in *The Silver Box*, 1909: 'He had a sensitive feeling for poetry and spectacle and romantic theatre'

his production of Galsworthy's *Loyalties*, for instance, could not have been better. When he directed *An Inspector Calls* by J. B. Priestley I was quite surprised to hear that both Alec Guinness and Ralph Richardson worked under him with the greatest respect and admiration. He certainly mellowed considerably as he got older.

In 1945, again under the auspices of ENSA, I made a five-month tour of India and the Far East, playing *Hamlet* and *Blithe Spirit* alternately for the troops. The first stop in our itinerary was a disused cinema in Bombay. We had a company of about twenty and brought our London costumes—which proved unwise as they were hot and cumbersome—and a minimum of scenery and lighting.

I was given a large bedroom at the Taj Mahal, a somewhat bleak but fairly luxurious hotel, sticky and clammy except for the dining room where the air conditioning and whirling fans suddenly struck one with a chilly blast. We rehearsed all day in the open-air cinema, sweating and cursing, while children swarmed outside, banging the walls with sticks, throwing pebbles and occasionally managing to sneak under a gate into the auditorium to peer and giggle at us as we worked. At the end of the exhausting afternoon I called the company on stage for notes, hastily taking off my doublet and shirt and putting on a very old, thin, white dressing-gown. Standing with my back to the auditorium, I was holding forth to the actors when I suddenly heard peals of laughter from the intruding children and, feeling something must be amiss, clapped my hands to my backside to find that the dressing gown had a gaping hole in the seat through which my black tights were plainly visible.

We were supposed to perform only for troops in uniform, but as the performance started that evening we saw that the front rows were occupied by turbaned Indians, several of them accompanied by saried ladies, who proved to be an admirably attentive and enthusiastic audience. The soldiers had evidently realized that intellectual Indians are devoted to Shakespeare and had flogged their tickets to advantage.

A night or two later we were all invited to a party at an Indian film studio and accepted without realizing that it was more than an hour's journey outside the city. We drove along apparently empty streets which seemed to be white with discarded newspapers. I was horrified to see these pale shapes materialize into beggars and vagrants, clad in dirty white rags which scarcely covered them. They rose from where they were lying and scattered in all directions as the car approached. When we finally reached the studio we were ushered, to our dismay, into a small projection-room where we had to endure three-quarters of an hour of an excruciatingly boring Indian film musical — mermaid princesses reclining on rocks in sub-aquatic settings and princes, with bows and arrows slung on their backs, diving to encounter them in amorous pursuit. Emerging from this exhausting spectacle, we found a huge buffet laid out and so much strong drink (which, of course, after wartime conditions in England and our recent hard night's work we could hardly wait to sample) that several members of the company collapsed immediately in a drunken stupor.

On the following afternoon I was lying naked on my bed in the hotel, trying to rest before my performance, when the telephone rang. A lady wished to see me urgently. I made excuses and declined politely but two minutes later my bedroom door was flung open by the manager with his pass-key and a voluminous female in purple muslin marched up to my bed as I hastily covered myself with the adjacent counterpane. 'I am Mrs Sabawala,' she announced. 'My house on Malabar Hill is a sermon in stone. You must lunch with me tomorrow. My car will call for you at one o'clock.' And she was gone without giving me time to protest.

Reluctantly, but secretly rather fascinated, I climbed into the car when it arrived next morning. Mrs Sabawala's house was large and imposing, with a crescent moon in cardboard attached to the front gate. There was a small party already assembled. The chairs were of black teak, without cushions, and consequently very hard to sit on. A small pool with a couple of rather sad lilies floating about in it occupied the centre of the room and I nearly tripped and fell into it as I retreated from a gentleman who rushed up to me to recite, at uncomfortably close quarters, a poem he had composed in my honour.

Mrs Sabawala turned out to be a very enthusiastic and successful amateur actress. She had lately scored a triumph as Madame Arcati in a local performance of *Blithe Spirit*. Her ambitions led her to hope she might come to England and try her fortunes on our stage — Equity, of course, permitting. She was extremely amiable and remorselessly pressing in her attempts to make me a party to her ambitions but I was not to be so easily persuaded. I never heard from her again.

In Bangalore we experienced charming hospitality from Ram

Gopal, the famous dancer. He knew London well as he had given some seasons there before the War and now came several times to see our *Hamlet*, sitting among the troops in his beautiful brocade coats of red or green. We were invited to his house—called 'Torquay Castle'—where statues of various Indian gods shared the place of honour with a large engraving of a Madonna bearing a bleeding heart. Mounting a steep outside staircase, he bade us remove our shoes as the room we were to visit was sacred to his mother. Here one of his aunts was sitting on the floor playing a large lute-like instrument and we listened politely, not quite knowing when the piece had finished or the appropriate moment at which we should be expected to applaud. On another evening, when we asked Gopal if he would not dance for us, he declined firmly but said his Guru would perform instead. We took our seats in a rather draughty courtyard with white walls and benches, rather like a fives court, where an orchestra of about eight persons, all of different ages, was already playing. A rather sinister figure was walking about behind the players drawing patterns on the floor in coloured chalks, reminding me forcibly of the vagrant who wanders in during the second act of *The Cherry Orchard*. Some time passed as the orchestra continued to play spasmodically. Then a very old gentleman, his body smeared with white streaks of paint and naked except for a loincloth, appeared and began to dance. We were told he was miming the god Shiva coming down from heaven and stealing the clothes of three maidens while they were bathing. We were duly impressed, though it was a cold night and we could not help wondering if the veteran performer managed to keep his circulation going more successfully than we did.

On another night at his house, Gopal at last consented to dance for us and retired to don his elaborate make-up and costume. He was away so long that most of the party had left before he finally appeared to delight the few of us who remained. The servants, who had hidden under the table-cloths, suddenly emerged to swell his rather scanty but enthusiastic audience.

A few days later Gopal kindly offered to take a group of us to Mysore in three cars and off we set, with Ram chattering gaily all the way, full of gossip about the London Theatre, which seemed unbelievably far off in such surroundings. The Mysore Palace was impressively elegant and massive, though somewhat unsuitably garnished with strings of coloured-glass lights left over from a recent festival. We became slightly hysterical when, as we were led to a

1 A portrait of Ellen Terry by her first husband, G. F. Watts. They first met when he was commissioned to paint her elder sister, Kate

2 & 3 Left: *Richard of Bordeaux*
at the New Theatre, 1933
4 Opposite: A costume design
for a Restoration piece,
by John Gielgud, 1922

5 Above: The programme for the Shakespeare Tercentenary
performance at Drury Lane, 1916
6 Below: Oscar Asche with his wife, Lily Brayton in his production of
Chu-Chin-Chow, which ran at His Majesty's from 1916 until 1921
7 Opposite: As Dostoevsky's *Grand Inquisitor* for the BBC/Open
University, 1976. Photograph by David Amy

8 Above: A design for Duke Frederick's Palace in *As You Like It*, by John Gielgud, 1916
9 Below: Directing a rehearsal of the Trial scene in *The Merchant of Venice* at the Old Vic, 1932, with Harcourt Williams (left, in dressing-gown) and Peggy Ashcroft as Portia (right centre, with arm raised). From a caricature by Roger K. Furse
10 & 11 Opposite: As Spooner in *No Man's Land* by Harold Pinter, and with Ralph Richardson as Hirst. From the Granada Television production, 1978

fenced enclosure to admire a group of magnificent sacred elephants, they all greeted our approach by getting erections and then urinating for several minutes in splashing streams.

In Madras, the theatre was a kind of Senate House with tiers of seats ascending to the roof in a semi-circle and an enormously wide orchestra pit between auditorium and stage. There was a monsoon raging outside and the rain lashed down so fiercely that we could hardly hear each other's voices as we tried to arrange the scenery and lighting. I realized immediately that we could never succeed in communicating *Hamlet* under such circumstances and, in a desperate flash of inspiration, enquired if the orchestra pit could not perhaps be boarded over. This was quite quickly done and I supervised a hasty rehearsal, moving all the action in front of the proscenium. The result was a very exciting performance. I was able to speak my soliloquies quite close to the audience, and made several effective entrances and exits through the gangways between the seats.

In Rangoon we played in a converted chapel with only a single row in the small gallery reserved for officers, and it was wonderful to find the non-commissioned audience so attentive and enthusiastic. I had feared they would want the conventional kind of troop entertainment, girls with concertinas, music and jolly jokes, but even if their initial motive for coming in was to take the weight off their feet, the entrance of the Ghost in the first scene of *Hamlet* seemed to awaken an interest which never faltered, even in the fairly long version which we played. It was well worth the trouble we had taken with our black curtains and simple but effective lighting; and our costumes were certainly impressive and decorative, however uncomfortable to wear in such a climate. I besought the actress who was playing Gertrude not to fling her heavy train to one side in the final scene, as clouds of dust flew up to choke me as I lay on the floor in the throes of approaching death. 'Oh, dear,' she said, 'I don't really feel like a Queen unless I can fling my train!'

One day we visited the Shwe Dagon Pagoda, a famous landmark of great antiquity and veneration. The central shrine was a huge copper dome within a railing, surrounded by a stone pavement and approached by a most imposing flight of steps. On each side of the stairs were stalls and shops with men in bowler hats and sarongs, some with cigars in their mouths, squabbling and bargaining and spitting scarlet betel juice in all directions, while mongrel dogs

12 John Gielgud in his country home. Photograph by Bernard Schwartz

barked and copulated and chased each other all over the shrine.

Singapore was dank and humid with forbidding Victorian architecture and statues. Staying at the famous Raffles Hotel, lately occupied by the Japanese who had left it in a state of considerable squalor, I woke in the middle of the night to find myself covered with strange white bites which had disappeared mysteriously by the time I woke up next morning. The theatre was large, with good acoustics, but as the windows had all been knocked out, the swifts, attracted by the lights, whirred noisily in and out all through the performances. The concert hall next door where the pianist Solomon was giving recitals, was equally windowless, so that applause or reactions in either auditorium disturbed any possibility of complete concentration in the other, though the enthusiastic audiences did not seem to mind as much as I did.

One night when I was not acting I went to the concert hall and stood at the back of the packed house to listen to an orchestra of soldiers recently released from prison camps, who were learning to recover their skills in playing instruments that they had not been able to touch for years. Behind me, in the harbour, was a line of dark battleships spread out under the night sky. It was extraordinary to hear a Beethoven symphony performed so movingly under such strange conditions.

The atmosphere of the Second War in London was a complete contrast to that of the First, when a tremendous number of revues were put on and *Chu-Chin-Chow* ran for years to an audience packed with khaki. In the Second War, with the Blitz and then the V1s and V2s, it was amazing that audiences came to the theatre at all, but there was a feeling of grim determination. I remember going to see *Swan Lake* at the Sadler's Wells Ballet one afternoon and watching the little swans doing their very intricate dance, crossing their feet, when suddenly a V2 went over. They tried not to look up into the air and we all held our breaths till the bomb burst somewhere on the other side of London. I remember lying on the stage, 'dead' in *Hamlet*, when a bomb was dropped into the Thames near the Savoy Hotel. Our scene-dock doors at the Haymarket Theatre in Suffolk Street burst open with a crash and a huge draught blew in. I thought

146

Macbeth, in my own production on tour in 1942, with Leon Quartermaine as the Ghost of Banquo

'Now we're really going to get it!' We felt that at any moment there might be fearful chaos in the theatre and people would be killed, but the audiences took it with amazing calm. There was no need for the sort of action my uncle Fred once had to take during the First War, when there was a Zeppelin raid and a bomb fell outside the theatre where he was playing in *The Scarlet Pimpernel*. He went down into the audience in his white satin coat, told the audience not to be frightened and then went back on stage and continued with the play.

Throughout the War years I never stopped working. When everyone else was having such a dreadful time I was extremely lucky to be doing the job I loved. In 1942 I played *Macbeth* for nearly a whole year, touring it and playing it in London in my own production. It was exhausting and not very successful, but ran quite a long time considering it is such a desperately difficult play and traditionally so very unlucky.

By 1944 I was pretty well exhausted, having directed a number of plays in which I did not act myself on top of my other commitments and then Hugh Beaumont[2] persuaded me to go into management again at the Haymarket and do five plays in repertoire—*Hamlet, Love for Love, The Circle, A Midsummer Night's Dream* and *The Duchess of Malfi*, with Peggy Ashcroft as leading lady.

I asked George Rylands, of Cambridge, to direct *Hamlet* and *The Duchess of Malfi* and later Nevill Coghill, of Oxford, to direct *A Midsummer Night's Dream*. I thought it would be interesting to have these distinguished University professors to work with, but I found that they did not get on very well with the actors and found it hard to understand their problems. They were used to students who obeyed them implicitly. The cast used to come to me and shake their heads and say 'You don't agree, do you? You don't think he's right?' It was awkward for me because I always felt the dons would think that I was trying to undermine their authority. All in all it was a somewhat tricky company, and at that stage of the War we were all feeling rather middle-aged and found that changing the bill and playing different parts was a strain. However, we plodded on and many people liked that last *Hamlet* better than any of my previous ones. I was happy to work with George Rylands whom I have always admired and liked very much. He was very strict over the text in both the plays he directed. I felt, though, that he did not watch the stage enough. He kept his eye on the book all the time and seemed to have little pictorial interest in the look of what was happening on

Oberon, with Peggy Ashcroft as Titania, in *A Midsummer Night's Dream*, Haymarket, 1944, directed by Nevill Coghill

Above: Valentine in *Love for Love*,
Phoenix and Haymarket, 1943-4.
And right: With Cecil Trouncer and D. J.
Williams. 'This scene, where Valentine
feigns lunacy, looks almost like a
reconstruction of a late eighteenth-
century painting by Robert Smirke,
although I had in fact not seen the
picture'

Duke Ferdinand in *The Duchess of Malfi*,
with Marian Spencer as Julia,
Haymarket, 1945, directed by George Rylands

the stage. In the *Dream* I felt that Nevill Coghill, with all his brilliant talent for outdoor theatre in Oxford, seemed penned in by the restrictions of the proscenium theatre. One should remember, however, that they were both still working at their universities and coming up on very slow, unheated trains every day to rehearsal.

It was during the run of *Love for Love* at the Haymarket that somebody told me one day that Shaw was in front. I could not imagine why—it was a matinée and I did not think he went to the theatre any more now that he was such an old man. Then I got a letter from him saying that he wanted me to play Caesar in the film of *Caesar and Cleopatra* with Vivien Leigh, which Gabriel Pascal was going to make. 'After all,' he said, 'I wrote the part of Caesar for Forbes-Robertson and it is in the great tradition of *Macbeth* and *Hamlet*. You'd be much better acting in it than playing a poor second-rate part in that eighteenth-century rubbish *Love for Love*.' I was highly flattered by this letter, but then I met Pascal and disliked him so much that I had the temerity to turn the part down, a decision which I rather regretted afterwards.

I have never done a great deal of Shaw. I have played two or three parts in filmed versions of *Saint Joan* at various times and the Inquisitor in a television version with Janet Suzman. At the Vic I played Sergius, and Marchbanks once at Oxford, but only for a week. I also played for a week the part of Dubedat, the painter, in a production of *The Doctor's Dilemma*, during the War when the actor who was officially playing it was ill. I played the Emperor in *Androcles* at the Vic and Shakespeare in *The Dark Lady of the Sonnets* but none of the major Shaw parts—except Shotover in *Heartbreak House* which I did for television. I am not enormously fond of Shaw's plays. I love reading them of course, and have hugely enjoyed watching them on the stage, but I have never longed to play any particular part.

Unfortunately, I only ever met Shaw to talk to once, at a very smart lunch party at Lady Colefax's, though on another occasion he came down to the Vic and read *Arms and the Man* to us in a mackintosh. He read with marvellous pace and skill and returned for the dress rehearsal. After the first act he called the actors together and gave them copious notes, but then he had to go off somewhere else for an appointment and as I did not come on until the second act he never saw me. In his notes he insisted on a lot of comic business—somebody throwing a coat to somebody and turning back at the exit to get a laugh. One can see in his plays that he often puts in gags and

153

Left: Captain Shotover in *Heartbreak House*, with Lesley-Ann Down as Ellie Dunn, BBC TV, 1977, produced by Cedric Messina comic nicknames to keep the audience awake in a long passage which he thinks might otherwise bore them. Another passion of his as a director was that he wanted actors to perform his plays as though they were musical scores.

Years later, Lady Astor, whom I had met on a boat coming back from America, offered to take me down to see him at Ayot St Lawrence and I was greatly tempted to accept. But Lady Astor was highly voluble and I was rather frightened of her. I thought two hours in a car with her, followed by an hour with Shaw during which I would have to break the ice with a man in his nineties, was too alarming a prospect. So I turned it down, which was stupid of me as I longed to see him and talk, especially about Ellen Terry.

Shaw's criticisms are probably the best in the world, with their shrewdness, wisdom, fun and wonderfully lively attitude to everything. I would have loved to have known him well. He was so kind to young people; he was wonderful to Coward, always giving him good advice, and he was very much more generous than people imagined. At the Everyman, Hampstead, where they did his plays in the twenties, he used to insist on his royalties — he thought it so important that authors should be protected over their rights — and then send them back under cover. It appeared that he was cruel to Mrs Patrick Campbell when she wrote begging for money in her last years, but she had behaved very tactlessly in reminding him of their abortive love-affair. She must have known how much he respected and admired his wife and that she had no business to publish his letters to her and make a fool of him before the world. I think he was quite justified in refusing to help her, though it was a sad situation, since he could obviously have afforded to help her if he had wanted to, and she certainly needed money very badly. Shaw was never afraid of public rows and he openly attacked Granville-Barker's departure from the stage, which upset Mrs Granville-Barker so much that Shaw and Granville-Barker were never to be friends again.

I find it interesting that he admired Chekhov so much. He said Chekhov's plays inspired him to write *Heartbreak House*, but that has always seemed to me a particularly bloodless play, a lot of eccentric characters flung together in a very absurd way, quite fun, but with none of the delicate subtlety of character that Chekhov's plays have. The only hint of Chekhov is that the play takes place in an old house in which a lot of crazy people live.

Now that he is dead the plays can be cut and are much better for it. In his lifetime he would never allow them to be cut at all in England. (He did not know that in America they were usually cut without acknowledgement). Shaw was always very interested in the actors and particularly the actresses who appeared in his plays. Everyone who was going to play St Joan was asked to go down to have an interview with him — Wendy Hiller, Katharine Cornell, Elisabeth Bergner—and they were all entertained and admonished. He loved to talk about the part and tell them how they ought to act it, and he was obviously a great actor himself. In the few news clips that remain you can hear the wonderful Irish accent and see the eyebrows shooting up and down.

Curiously enough, just as my memory of the beginning of the War is linked with Granville-Barker, so is that of the end of it. He and his wife came to dinner with me the night peace was declared. I had just played *Hamlet* in London for the last time, and I knew that they had been to see the play. But Granville-Barker refused to talk about the theatre at dinner. Instead, his wife chattered about her dog which was in quarantine, some Spanish poetry which she had translated and all sorts of other things. However, after dinner, when we went upstairs, Granville-Barker took me into a corner. Having thanked him for the help he had given me in the Elsinore *Hamlet* I told him that there were certain things I did not like about the current production. 'In my first scene I have to sit on the stage looking at the audience, whereas you made me come late to the council table and doodle on my papers and fidget—it was so much more original and effective.' Granville-Barker replied 'Oh I'm afraid we didn't see the first act because we were late, we'd had a late lunch.' This upset me, rather naturally. He began to look very sleepy and soon after he and his wife left in a taxi. About a week later he wrote me a charming letter in which he said some very nice things about my Hamlet; but he would never have been late for the first act of *Hamlet* in the old days.

CHAPTER
SIX

1946–1954

By the end of the War I was pretty well tired out. I had fulfilled so many of my youthful ambitions that I did not know where to go. I had a fairly bad patch for a few years when I did not choose plays particularly well and my luck seemed to have run out. I did a version of *Crime and Punishment* in 1946, for instance, that was fairly interesting, but I was really too old for Raskolnikov. Many times in my career I have been bothered about the question of age, though I cannot help admiring old actors who can still give an impression of youth. Leon Quartermaine, for example, who became a great friend of mine and was a most beautiful artist, acted with me in Congreve's *Love for Love* when he was nearly seventy and hardly used any make-up at all. He played the part of a young rake with such charm and style that you never noticed that he was much too old for it. On the other hand I think it is dangerous to encourage very young people to rush into parts like Romeo and Juliet just because they are in fact thirteen and fourteen. Of course my own first Romeo, at nineteen, had been more or less a disaster!

Just after the War, in 1947, I went to the States with *The Importance of Being Earnest* and *Love for Love*. *The Importance* was an enormous success but the Americans did not take to *Love for Love* at all. It was not perhaps as well played as in London. We had been acting it for a long time in England and I think I had become stale. The same thing happened later with *Much Ado* which I had done three times in

England before I took it to New York. *The Importance* stood up to new rehearsals, but *Love for Love* did not. I think, too, that Americans find it difficult to accept the sort of debauched aristocratic society that Congreve draws so well. They also find the very long sentences and archaic language difficult to understand. The Victorian era of *The Importance* is much more familiar, Wilde did, after all, go to America himself on lecture tours and his play has always been a success there.

I take some pride in the fact that, after our revival with Edith Evans as Lady Bracknell at the beginning of the War, nobody put on *The Importance* for some ten years. That is one of the tests of a successful production. It shows that you have made a definitive mark with a certain play. The same thing happened with *Much Ado* and it gave me much satisfaction.

The Importance of Being Earnest has to be played very strictly; it is like chamber music. You must not indulge yourself, or caricature. You must play it with your tongue in your cheek, like a solemn charade. The muffin scene, for instance, very easily degenerates into a knock-about. I discovered this years after I thought I had finished with the play for ever. Robert Flemyng and I were asked to do the second act at a benefit in Oxford. We rehearsed it again and I said. 'I believe I've been wrong about this scene whenever I have played it. I think it must be acted very slowly.' We began rehearsing it at half the pace and got many, many more laughs out of it by eating the muffins with real solemnity. Edith Evans always played Lady Bracknell in a very deliberate manner without any sense of urgency or crisis. My mother once said to me, 'Your generation will never understand the meaning of leisure. We used to spend whole afternoons driving round the park, leaving cards turned down at the edges on people we'd had dinner with the week before.' Even in my own youth there seemed to be so much more time for everything although, of course, many things took much longer. Love affairs carried on during the afternoon must have been more than usually time-consuming when you think of the amount of clothes that had to be taken off and put on again before the participants could reappear downstairs for their five-course dinner.

I remember doing pieces of Sheridan and Congreve at my drama schools and finding the plays very difficult to read. When we came to revive *Love for Love* I discovered that I remembered some of the lines from 1924 when I had played Valentine at Oxford. I had seen one revival of the play by Guthrie, with Charles Laughton and Athene

Seyler, at Sadler's Wells in 1934, and I remembered that Valentine's mad scene was fun to play. When I suggested doing it to Binkie Beaumont in 1943, he rather jumped at the idea. Beaumont was a very clever man. At a dress rehearsal he knew exactly what to say. Although Shakespeare and Congreve were not really up his street—he was a modern man with no pretensions to education at all and no knowledge except what he had learnt as he became success-ful—he immediately put his finger on what was wrong, advising us on cuts and all sorts of other details that were admirably constructive and not in the least discouraging. I always trusted his judgement. He would leave me alone until a very late stage in production and would then say just two or three things at the last moment which were extremely helpful.

The great exponent of Restoration comedy was Edith Evans. Nobody could touch her in parts like Millamant in *The Way of the World*. This is a cumbrous and difficult play—Millamant really has only three good scenes in it—and while Lady Wishfort is fun, the plot is a frightful bore. In *Love for Love*, the balance is more attractive. There are about eight good parts in it, whereas in *The Way of the World* the majority of the parts, except for Millamant and Lady Wishfort, are feeble and by no means easy to cast. I had a wonderful team when we performed *Love for Love*—Yvonne Arnaud, Cecil Trouncer, Miles Malleson, Leon Quartermaine and Leslie Banks, all dyed-in-the-wool professionals who had been in the theatre for so many years that they brought great experience to the work. But in *The School for Scandal*, which I directed many years later, the cast was far less evenly balanced. The difficulty is to find the actors to play Charles and Joseph Surface. Also, the action is divided all through into different sections which the director must try to weld together somehow.

When I came back from the 1947 tour of America, I was told about a play called *The Lady's Not for Burning* which had been done in my absence by Alec Clunes at the Arts Theatre. I found out that Clunes, who was running the theatre at that time, had paid Christopher Fry a bursary for a year to write the play for him. Clunes had acted in it and directed it but nobody could decide whether it had any sort of chance with an ordinary public. After its short run at the Arts Theatre, where it had had encouraging

Left: Raskolnikov in *Crime and Punishment*, New and Globe Theatres, 1946, directed by Anthony Quayle

Right: Thomas Mendip in my own production of Christopher Fry's *The Lady's Not for Burning*, with Pamela Brown and Richard Burton, Globe, 1949

Below: *The Lady's Not for Burning*, 1949. From left to right: David Evans, Richard Leech, Claire Bloom, Nora Nicholson, myself, Eliot Makeham, Harcourt Williams, Pamela Brown

notices, Clunes suddenly decided to sell the play, and I was asked if I would be interested to which I replied that I had not even read it yet. I was going down to see some play at Cambridge with Binkie Beaumont and I read the first act in the train. I threw it across to Beaumont and said 'I must do this play. You must get it for me.' And he did.

We took nearly a year to put it on because Pamela Brown was not available. Fry had worked a great deal with her at Oxford during the War—where she had made great successes as Hedda and in various other parts—and he was determined that she should play the part of Jennet, the supposed witch. When it came to casting the boy, Beaumont had no doubts: 'We must have Richard Burton of course.' I said 'Who's he?'

Richard had just made a great success in Emlyn Williams' *The Druid's Rest*. He turned up at rehearsal the next day and I realized that he was perfect for the part. I never had to tell him anything at all, except not to yawn so much when he wanted his lunch.

Esmé Percy played the tinker who had one scene in the last act. He was a delightful man.[1] He had played nearly all the big Shaw parts, touring for years with the MacDona Company. He had been very handsome until one of his eyes was bitten out by a dog and his nose was disfigured in another accident. He was odd-looking when I knew him, short and rather stout, but he had the most entrancing generosity and sweetness and was a very clever, volatile actor. I asked him to help me direct *The Lady's Not for Burning*, which he did, and he was very good in his one scene at the end, though he used to amuse himself with all sorts of business and antics. He had worked with Bernhardt as a young man, and he told me that he had to leave her company because she said he was getting too much like her! Indeed, he could imitate her brilliantly and told wonderful stories about her. He was the actor who, in the heyday of his good looks, was asked by Herbert Tree to supper one night after the play by himself. Lady Tree is said to have looked in at the door and said: 'The port's on the sideboard, Herbert, and remember it's adultery just the same!' One night during his big scene in *The Lady* his glass eye fell out. We were all transfixed with horror but Richard Leech, who was a doctor as well as acting in the play, had the presence of mind to step forward and pick it up. Esmé was saying under his breath 'Oh, do be careful, don't tread on it, they cost £8 each.' After that I persuaded him to wear a patch, which he did rather reluctantly.

He was very much the old-fashioned English gentleman. When we were on tour in America—he was then in his seventies—he used to ring me up at nine in the morning and tell me he had been made an honorary member of some distinguished club in Boston or Washington, and he would invite me to lunch and then have some famous house opened specially for us to go to see. We used to go down to Greenwich Village after the theatre and he would have lots of young people sitting round him at supper listening to his stories. He still loved animals, particularly dogs, in spite of his accident, and when he died, the night before he was to have opened in a play in Brighton, they found him in his hotel, dead in bed, with his last dog lying on his lap.

I managed to persuade Christopher Fry to make a few minor changes and cuts in the play and clarify some lines while we were on tour. In rehearsal I would go out front to watch my understudy walking my part so that I could see where I had to be in a scene—and very often I would find I had put myself in the wrong place and would have to change things round. We rehearsed the play most thoroughly and when we opened in London it became a huge success and ran for a year. When we took it to America it was equally successful—the text was still in the best-seller list of the *New York Times* the week our production closed.

After the long years of the war it was curious how T. S Eliot and Fry both had a few years of great theatrical success with modern verse plays. People seemed to long to hear modern verse spoken again on the stage.

The audiences liked the romance and colour of *The Lady's Not for Burning*; there had not been a costume play in London for a long time and Oliver Messel had done a most beautiful décor for it—a little too beautiful I thought afterwards. I had an idea that if it had been staged in modern dress perhaps the meaning of the play would have been clearer. Christopher Fry had been a conscientious objector and his views were reflected in the character I played, a soldier returning from the war, wanting to be hanged in his disillusionment. I thought that if he had come back in battle-dress, the disowned son of a gentleman who had joined up in the ranks, the message might have been clearer.

I got on better with Christopher Fry than I did with T. S. Eliot. In some way I seemed to alarm him. In 1939 I had intended to direct and act the leading part in *The Family Reunion*, which had intrigued me, though I did not understand it very well. I had lined up a wonderful cast—Dame May Whitty, Sybil Thorndike, Martita Hunt—and had scheduled the play for matinées at the Globe Theatre. I was then asked to go to meet Eliot for the first time at the Reform Club. To my surprise he was a rather sober-looking gentleman in a black coat and striped trousers. We had oysters, I remember, and it was very formal. I was rather nervous and began to draw patterns on the table cloth. 'Should the set be like this?' I asked him. 'The French windows, should they be there!' and 'How do you want the Eumenides to be seen? Or should they be invisible, or perhaps in masks?' The more I talked, the more silent Eliot became. However, I left thinking that I had created quite a good impression. I continued to think so until, a few days later, I met Sybil Thorndike who said 'You know, Eliot's not going to let you have his play—he says you have no faith.' Evidently he feared I was going to turn it into a fashionable Shaftesbury Avenue comedy, though he never wrote to me to explain his decision,

Many years later I went to Marrakesh for a holiday and found that Eliot was staying in the same hotel with his second wife. He was already ill—it was not long before his death. I spoke to him and said how sorry I was I had not done *Family Reunion*, but he still did not reveal what he had felt about me or why he had turned me down. I said I had played in it on the radio with some success and had made a recording of his *Journey of the Magi* which people liked. He asked me to send it to him, and he wrote me a very nice letter about it. I am sure that, over *The Family Reunion*, he had found me over-assertive—perhaps he was right.

My 1949 production of *Much Ado*, at Stratford-on-Avon, with Anthony Quayle and Diana Wynyard as Benedick and Beatrice, was very successful indeed. The whole cast worked wonderfully together and I engaged an enchanting designer called Mariano Andreu, a Spaniard, whom I discovered more or less by accident. I had been to see a ballet by Michel Fokine at the old Alhambra Theatre in Leicester Square, and had never forgotten the marvellous sets. There were white curtains with black and red motifs on them, rather like an Aubrey Beardsley. Four women, who looked enormously tall, came on and drew the curtains aside to reveal beautiful insets of palaces and gardens. When it came to *Much Ado* I thought that I must find the same designer. Somebody told me that he had recently designed a three-act play be Montherlant called *Le Maître de Santiago* in Paris. I rushed over to Paris, but in the lobby of the hotel where I was staying there was a poster advertising *Le Maître de Santiago* and, pasted over it, a slip saying the performances were cancelled because the leading man was ill, so I never saw Andreu's scenery for this play, but I did discover the man himself in the end. He came over to England and we worked together happily on *Much Ado* and, later, *The Trojans* at Covent Garden. He was an elderly man, sixty I suppose, very amusing, but speaking little English. We had endless discussions with diagrams and pantomime and he produced wonderful designs for *Much Ado*. I had always been obsessed by the photographs of Christian Bérard's designs for Louis Jouvet's production of Molière's *L'Ecole des Femmes*, in which a series of walls showed the street outside and then opened out like screens to show the garden. Mariano saw just what I meant at once and he devised for me a kind of picture-book garden setting for *Much Ado*, very simple though extremely decorative. Eight pages came on at the end of the scenes and turned the walls and the garden became a ballroom and later on, a church.

Much Ado was interesting for me for another reason. I have acted Benedick with three different Beatrices. At Stratford in 1950, Peggy Ashcroft played the part and in the London production Diana Wynyard took it on. I was afraid Peggy would be disappointed, but fortunately she and Diana were great friends and there was no awkwardness. I played it again with Peggy a few years later, and when I took the play to America in 1959 Margaret Leighton was Beatrice—and absolutely enchanting too. But by that time I thought my production had become rather old-fashioned. They reproduced the scenery poorly and it was not well lit. It looked like a Soho trattoria and lacked the lovely classical Italian quality that it had in England.

Peggy Ashcroft's Beatrice was most original. Diana Wynyard played it much more on the lines that I imagine Ellen Terry did —the great lady, sweeping about in beautiful clothes. When Peggy started rehearsing, she rather jibbed at all that and said 'I'm not going to wear those dresses, they're too grand for me.' She evolved her own approach to the character, just as good as Diana's but

Benedick, in the 1952 production of *Much Ado About Nothing*, at the Phoenix, with Diana Wynyard as Beatrice: 'The great lady, sweeping about in beautiful clothes'

Benedick, with Peggy Ashcroft as Beatrice, in my own production of *Much Ado About Nothing*, Stratford-on-Avon, 1950. 'A touch of Beatrice Lillie'

totally different—almost with a touch of Beatrice Lillie. She wore much simpler dresses and created a cheeky character who means well but seems to drop bricks all the time (perhaps she got it from me). Everybody thinks Beatrice will never marry because she is too free with her tongue and is rather impertinent to people without intending any rudeness.

As far as my own performance was concerned over the years I kept trying to make Benedick into more of a soldier. At first Mariano encouraged me to be a dandy, wearing comic hats, one like a blancmange, another with a round brim trimmed with feathers. The hats used to get laughs the moment I came on in them. I decided that this had not much to do with Shakespeare's play, so I gradually discarded them and wore leather doublets and thigh boots and became less of the courtier. I tried to inject a good deal more bluffness and strength into the part. Benedick ought to be an uncouth soldier, a tough misanthrope, who wears a beard and probably smells to high heaven. When this went against the grain I tried to console myself with the idea that Irving must have been more of the courtier too, but of course I never saw his performance. I saw the play once with my uncle Fred as Benedick, but by then he was too old for it and he did comic tricks like hiding in a tree in the orchard scene and falling out of it. He was very fat and a bit more like Falstaff than Benedick, though he was, as always, wonderful in the love scenes with his tenderness and his lovely voice.

Much Ado has been an enormous success in very varied productions since the 1950s. There was the Zeffirelli version with statues that came to life and Albert Finney in a Mexican get-up smoking a cigar, and one with an Indian setting with Judi Dench and Donald Sinden. Michael Redgrave and Googie Withers played it at Stratford in Victorian clothes, which Edith Evans assured me was brilliant. But I have never wanted to see *Much Ado* in Victorian or Edwardian costume, because I do not think those fashions can ever suit a play which is so full of Elizabethan sex jokes. The jokes are hardly credible when set in a period in which everybody was ashamed to show so much as an ankle.

Personally, I do not like Shakespeare to be acted in any period later than Jacobean, because it seems to me that if you are playing in Restoration costume with big wigs, or in eighteenth-century dresses with white wigs and high heels, or in Victorian strapped trousers and frock coats, you cannot sit or stand appropriately to match the text.

King Lear, Stratford-on-Avon, 1950, directed by Anthony Quayle and myself. The reconciliation scene with Andrew Cruickshank (Kent) and Peggy Ashcroft (Cordelia).

    Be your tears wet? Yes, faith. I pray you, weep not.
    if you have poison for me I will drink it.
    I know you do not love me; for your sisters Have, as I do remember, done me wrong: You have some cause, they have none

Left: The Noguchi *King Lear*, directed by George Devine and myself, with Japanese décor, Palace, 1955. Claire Bloom as Cordelia

You can, of course, avoid costume altogether and use modern dress, but I find it confusing. Guthrie did Edwardian productions of *All's Well that Ends Well, Hamlet* and *Troilus and Cressida*. I was unfamiliar with *Troilus* and could not follow the play properly, being unable to distinguish between the Greeks and the Trojans. Of course, *Antony and Cleopatra,* and the other Roman plays, and even *Macbeth*, were originally done in Elizabethan clothes with a few extra touches to give an idea of period. Probably the Elizabethan audience would have accepted very simple suggestions—a Roman helmet or a toga thrown over a doublet—enough to give a feeling of ancient Rome or Egypt. I was once very rash when I asked Noguchi to design *King Lear* for me in 1955. His Japanese costumes killed all our efforts to act in them. There were very interesting things about the production, but it was hopeless from the costume point of view, and I remember saying at the dress rehearsal to George Devine, who was directing it with me, 'Can't we scrap all the costumes and just have rubber sheets with holes for our heads?'

Costumes in correct period can be a problem for an actor. But designers are determined to have their own way and they are quite right. I remember in *Love for Love* I had the luck to persuade Rex Whistler, who was to be killed so tragically in France on D-Day, to do the scenery. He was training in the Guards and could not get much time off, so he was unable to design the costumes and I therefore engaged a wonderful elderly lady called Jeanetta Cochrane. (The theatre at the Central School of Art and Design in Holborn is named after her.) She was rather jolly and red-faced, like an admiral's daughter, and when we went for the first fittings to Simmonds the costumiers, who were supposed to be the best in London, she said 'Oh, that coat is not cut right at all, the shoulders shouldn't be like that, they shouldn't be padded, that's not in my design.' The cutter was furious and said 'How dare you speak to me like that? I have just done 350 dresses for Mr Ivor Novello and he was delighted with them.' 'Well,' Miss Cochrane replied, 'old Monsieur Leloi trained me and I happen to know that the shoulders should be this way.' 'Monsieur Leloi! He is my god,' cried the cutter, and Miss Cochrane had her way.

If given a chance, costumiers will often take short cuts, and actors and actresses too can be very difficult about their costumes. The high heels and heavy coats for men in eighteenth-century plays alter your balance, and actresses used to be very reluctant to wear tight corsets, although the young actresses today seem to be very good about it all. I have noticed in the last few years how they all wear the correct corsets and petticoats, perhaps because television and films insist on greater accuracy. Edith Evans was exceptional, as she always said she could not play a costume part unless she was dressed absolutely in the right period, right down to the underclothes. Nowadays, directors are also anxious that the actors and actresses should have some rough idea of what they are going to wear at rehearsal so that they can get used to it.

In 1950 I had what amounted to a fresh start in a glorious season at Stratford, playing four parts—Angelo, Cassius, Benedick and King Lear. It was meeting Peter Brook at Stratford and doing *Measure for Measure* with him that really started me off on this new line of work. I had seen *Measure for Measure* with Charles Laughton in the early thirties at the Old Vic in a production with Flora Robson and James Mason that Guthrie had done. It was the best production of that season. Most of the other plays were less successful because Laughton was not really very good in any of them. But he was wonderful as Angelo and I remember thinking that this highly unsympathetic character, a self-righteous prig, was one I could play—perhaps there was a bit of my own nature in it. Angelo, and afterwards Leontes (in which Peter Brook directed me too) were great challenges for me, though I have always thought I was rather good in unsympathetic parts—in *The Circle*, for instance, as the husband who likes the antique furniture better than his young wife, and in *A Day by the Sea*, in which I was the dreary son of the house who is an ineffectual civil servant. If you play someone who is not very agreeable, you do not try to make him sympathetic, but you do try to make him amusing and interesting. Bores, after all, are interesting phenomena in that they themselves do not think that they are bores at all.

Peter Brook has become something of a legend now, but in the 1950s at Stratford he was still very young, approachable and jolly.[2] Like Komisarjevsky he did everything himself, designed the scenery, found the music, controlled the lighting. His *A Midsummer Night's Dream* was extraordinary, I thought. He is also an enchanting companion and we have always liked each other. Some actors find him unsympathetic, even somewhat severe, but I would do anything he asked me. I trust him entirely for his beautiful taste and marvellous imagination.

Peter has great respect for the text, especially in Shakespeare, though lately he seems to have worked more enthusiastically with improvised texts or even (as Craig used to suggest as an ideal) with no text at all. He does not mess about with the lines, and he does try to work with his actors. I used to stop in the middle of rehearsing Leontes or Angelo and say 'I don't understand this speech at all, Peter,' and he would break off the rehearsal and go into a corner to discuss it with me for ten minutes. He is enormously thorough and full of inspiration.

He and I did the Seneca *Oedipus* together at the National Theatre in 1968 and had an exhausting time preparing it. Nowadays, Peter will not even design the set until he has started work with the actors. In *Oedipus* the management was very upset because he would not decide what we were to wear or what scenery was to be built. Peter enjoys his authority: he would walk into the rehearsal room and say curtly 'No newspapers!', and every morning the whole cast had to do exercises. It was rather like being in the Army and I dreaded it; but at the same time I knew I wanted to be a part of such an experiment. Peter Brook battered me down to my lowest ebb during the rehearsals, saying 'You can't do that, it's awfully false and theatrical', and giving me extraordinarily difficult things to do. In the big scene, when I discovered what had happened—that I had killed my father and married my mother—I had to deliver a highly emotional speech kneeling on the ground, then get up quietly and go to sit at the side of the stage on a stool with the chorus, quite impassively, while the messenger came on and described me putting my eyes out. At the end of his ten-minute monologue, I had to get up from my stool (I was dressed in slacks and a jersey) and go into the voice and manner of the blinded Oedipus, trying to produce my voice in a strange strangled tone which Peter had invented at rehearsal with endless experiment. Technically, that was one of the most difficult things that I have ever done in my life—very good, I suppose, for my ego.

I have always been sorry that there was no record of *Oedipus*, either on disc or film, because not only the look, but the sound of it was so impressive. The chorus was disposed in the most original way, with some of the actors tied to posts around the pillars of the auditorium. (Latecomers were sometimes known to ask them for programmes.)

Angelo in *Measure for Measure*,
1950, directed by Peter Brook

Cassius in *Julius Caesar*, 1950,
directed by Anthony Quayle and
Michael Langham

Benedick in *Much Ado About
Nothing*, 1950, directed by myself

King Lear, 1950, directed by myself
and Anthony Quayle
'In 1950 I had what amounted to a
fresh start in a glorious season at
Stratford, playing four parts –
Angelo, Cassius, Benedick and King
Lear'

There was one chorus, when Icarus falls from the sky, where the voices came from high up in the top gallery, passed down the circles and then were taken up by the actors on stage. The effect was like the great picture by Breughel with the boy falling into the water.

After Stratford I worked with Peter again in my own season at the Lyric Theatre, Hammersmith in the year I was knighted, 1953. We had opened with *Richard II*. I decided I was too old to play Richard myself and rather regretted it afterwards—and followed with *The Way of the World* and Otway's *Venice Preserv'd*, which Peter was to direct. I directed *The Way of the World* and *Richard II* in which Paul Scofield gave a fine performance, though I do not think I helped him very much. I was too aware that I had played the part myself and that I was not giving him a sufficiently free hand to develop it along his own lines. He is a very individual actor in that he seldom feels really confident in his performance until just before the first night. Peter Brook, who has worked with him a great deal, told me that in *The Power and the Glory*, in which he was to give such a superb performance, he came to life only at the last dress rehearsal when everybody was in complete despair and thought the play was going to be a failure.

In *The Way of the World* I could not find much to do with Mirabell and was haunted by the memory of Edith Evans' performance as Millamant, which was perhaps why I failed to help Pamela Brown, whom I loved and who had made such a great success with me in *The Lady's Not for Burning*. The success of the production was chiefly due to Margaret Rutherford's splendid Lady Wishfort. The charming décor was designed by James Bailey and I managed to arrange the text a little better than usual to simplify the rather boring complications.

I had read *Venice Preserv'd* some years before and felt there was something strikingly effective in the play, and Peter Brook agreed. Nobody had done it since the eighteenth century, when all the great actors and actresses had played it, but it seemed tailor-made for me and Scofield—one of the few plays, like *Othello*, which has two magnificent leading parts for men. Beaumont liked it but we both realized it needed a certain amount of doctoring. So Peter Brook and I did a little work on the text. Leslie Hurry was engaged to do the décor, which was beautiful, very simple. The cast included Eileen Herlie, Pamela Brown, Scofield, myself and Herbert Lomas, a fine old character actor. It was really a great success all round though,

Leontes in *The Winter's Tale*, Phoenix, 1951, directed by Peter Brook oddly enough, of the three productions that season it was the only one that lost money.[3]

Later in 1953, I decided to take the production of *Richard II* to Bulawayo, where I had been asked to appear at the Rhodes Festival. I thought it would be an opportunity to play Richard for the last time, out of London. We took the play out with the scenery we had used at Hammersmith, little realizing that when we got to Bulawayo we would have to perform it in a vast theatre, part of a huge exhibition built on a windswept plain. The stage was enormously wide and when we put up our poor little scenery from the Lyric it looked like a child's plaything. It was July, but freezing cold, and the audience sat with rugs over them. Fortunately, our costumes were fairly thick. Very few people came to the Festival, everything was very expensive, the hotel was horrible—only two spoons to be found in the whole establishment. After the show we had to eat in the streets, hot dogs by the light of paraffin lamps, because nobody would stay up to give us any supper when we got back and the night club was too expensive. At the end of the four week run I went off to the game reserves for a holiday. I shall never forget the Victoria Falls, especially from the air, as our plane flew over them, and Rhodes' impressive tomb, hidden away in the depths of the country.

In 1955 I directed *Twelfth Night* at Stratford with Vivien Leigh as Viola and Laurence Olivier as Malvolio. Somehow the production did not work, I do not know why. *Twelfth Night* must be one of the most difficult plays to direct, though it is one of my favourites. I have seen so many bad productions and never a perfect one. I would give anything to have seen Granville-Barker's. In the first one I ever saw—Fagan's at the Court many years ago—the only memorable performance was by Arthur Whitby, a splendid actor, now forgotten, who played Sir Toby Belch. I acted Malvolio once at Sadler's Wells with Ralph Richardson as Sir Toby and enjoyed it, though that production was not very good either. It is so difficult to combine the romance of the play with the cruelty of the jokes against Malvolio, jokes which are in any case archaic and difficult. The different elements in the play are hard to balance properly. At Stratford I know that the actors were not very happy with my production, partly because of the scenery, which was too far up-stage. I thought Vivien Leigh was enchanting—though the critics did not care for her very much—but she was torn between what I was trying to make her do and what Olivier thought she should do, while Olivier was set on

Above: Mirabell in my production of *The Way of the World*, Lyric, 1953
Right: Jaffier in Peter Brook's production of *Venice Preserv'd*, Lyric, 1953

playing Malvolio in his own particular rather extravagant way. He was extremely moving at the end, but he played the earlier scenes like a Jewish hairdresser, with a lisp and an extraordinary accent, and he insisted on falling backwards off a bench in the garden scene, though I begged him not to do it. I had not directed him since the days we had done *Romeo and Juliet* together and he was inclined to be obstinate. But then Malvolio is a very difficult part. The problem is to combine the dignity of the character with the fun and to make the tragic end, when he is put in the madhouse, succeed.

In 1952, I had directed Ralph Richardson in *Macbeth* but that too was not at all a success. I enjoyed the production if only because I also designed the scenery which I thought was pretty effective, though rather obvious too, consisting mostly of black velvet. This worked much better than the Arthurian medieval scenery I had used in my own production in 1942, which was picturesque but did not help the play very much. At Stratford I had a pitch-dark stage with very strong lights on the actors and the scene of Birnam Wood coming to Dunsinane worked rather well, as did the apparitions. On the whole, however, the production was a great disappointment both for Ralph and myself. I was sorry I had not managed to make it a success; perhaps *Macbeth* really is an ill-fated play. When I did it in the War three people died during the tour. There must be something in the legend of the curse.

I would like to have been clever enough to design more productions myself. I have always had a very strong feeling for the space on the stage, and I found that when I came to work as a director with designers it was fascinating to see how quickly the good ones recognized areas of the stage which could be used in different scenes to break up the monotony of a conventional square scene. At Barnes when I worked with Komisarjevsky on a tiny cinema-type stage he did some brilliantly inventive sets for *Three Sisters* and *Katerina*. In the latter play he broke up the stage space and cut a trap-door in the middle of the floor, through which we made our entrances in the studio scene. The furniture was angled obliquely from the audience and I realized the possibilities open to a clever director for interesting grouping, how the actors can be raised at some points and lowered at others.

Then I went through a period of wanting pretty picture scenery, and the productions I did at the Queen's Theatre in 1937 were fairly decorative, though simple and not spectacular. They were an attempt to give the Motleys, who did *Bordeaux* for me so beautifully, a chance to develop their gifts. In the late 1940s there was a period of elaborate scenery at Stratford and James Bailey, Leslie Hurry and a number of delightful designers did beautiful décors at different times. I do not think now they would suit the feeling of the theatre today. John Bury has lately produced quite different kinds of settings for the classics though, of course, even he owes something to some of the best designers of the past—Lovat Fraser, Gordon Craig, even Bibiena.

In the past ten years the designers have been experimenting a great deal with the floors of their settings. I think a sloped stage can often be very effective though it can also be very awkward for the actors. When I was young a lot of the stages were already raked—the Haymarket, for instance. In Peter Hall's production of *The Tempest* at the Old Vic by John Bury, the rake was so steep that I could hardly keep my balance on it. It is difficult to realize, unless you have been an actor for many years, particularly in Shakespeare, how important it is to have a firm floor under your feet to keep your balance. When I played Hamlet in America I was given a beautiful set with two flights of steps; but there were so many that I spent my whole time with one foot up and the other down, which was terribly tiring. When you are speaking very long, elaborate speeches, it is vital to be comfortably balanced, especially in the classics, where so much is spoken standing. Marie Tempest always insisted, even in a modern play, that every sofa she acted on had boards under the cushions. She would never have a soft piece of furniture to sit on because it was not possible to keep a dignified stance—she was very small—and push her voice out.

One designer who always fascinated me from boyhood was Edward Gordon Craig, the illegitimate son of Ellen Terry and the architect and designer Edward Godwin. He wanted not only to conceive the production and to design the scenery, but also to do the lighting, cast the play and direct everybody. I suppose the fact that he himself had failed as an actor made him contemptuous of the way the London theatre was run commercially. He used his mother very

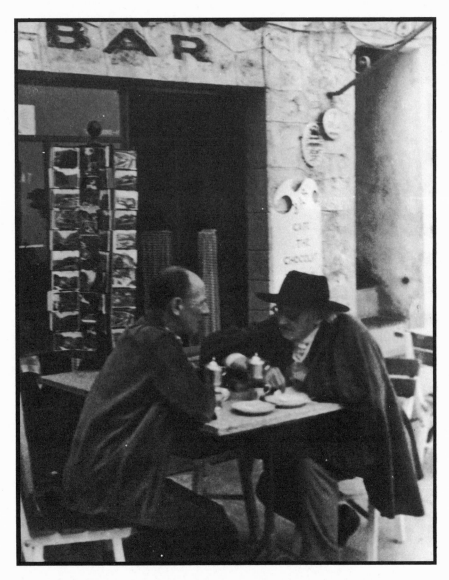

With Edward Gordon Craig in Vence, Summer 1953. Opposite above: Craig as
Arviragus in *Cymbeline* at the Lyceum in 1896, when he appeared with his mother,
Ellen Terry, and Henry Irving. Below: Craig in his nineties

unintelligently when she offered to back him at the Imperial Theatre in 1901. He persuaded her to do Ibsen's *The Vikings of Heligoland* and play a part quite unsuited to her, and she had to put on a revival of *Much Ado* to replace it. Craig exhausted all the money she had saved to put it on.

His strongest influence, undoubtedly, has been by proxy, in the effect he has had on other designers and directors; and I think he knew it. He was a jealous, slightly bitter man and yet very funny. He inherited Ellen Terry's sense of humour which made him very amusing company, although he did not seem to have a grain of humour in his love affairs—especially the famous episode with Isadora Duncan. He treated women in a cavalier fashion deserting them when they found themselves inconveniently pregnant. He had various children all over Europe and was very strict with them when they lived with him, getting them up at five in the morning to clean his brushes and sweep his studio. When I knew him he was a very old man but still in wonderful spirits. He had no teeth but ate enormous meals and chattered away, looking picturesquely sly and coy and nodding, like an old raven, with his head on one side. He refused to learn any languages; though he lived in Italy and France most of his life, he went on speaking English and managed to make himself understood somehow.

He was surprisingly knowledgeable about what was going on in the theatre all over Europe. He went to see Olivier in *Richard III* in Paris and admired him greatly. The only time he visited England in my day was in 1930, at the invitation of C. B. Cochran, the great British impresario, just after I had made my first success at the Old Vic.

He was rather patronizing when we lunched together and I found him a disappointment. He did no work at all, left unpaid bills behind and really behaved, as usual, pretty badly. He was irresistible all the same. I could understand why Ellen Terry worshipped him. How she must have longed to help him, knowing his ideas were thrilling and before their time. She would have liked to help him to make a financial success out of them. She also sympathized with all his discarded lovers—she had been unlucky in love herself after all—and always kept in touch with them, giving them money for themselves and their children. Craig became more and more a cracky, curious genius, a sort of scandal to the whole of Europe. He enjoyed becoming a legend, but he was too suspicious to let anybody manage him or help him to carry out his ideas and to solidify the promise of his drawings and essays.

There are times when I think I have made a reasonable success as a director. I would not want to direct Shakespeare now because I think my methods are probably out of date. I would perhaps be adequate to direct a perfectly straight play, knowing how to group the people and put over the points correctly, but as a director I have never, I think, been able to put any great personal stamp on a play.

It is difficult to tell exactly what the director does unless you have been at every rehearsal. Ordinary playgoers do not appreciate the amount of compromise, the coaxing, the occasional ill-feeling and the numerous changes of direction which a play may take in the course of rehearsals. The actors are the only ones who really know what the director has contributed to a play. For many years I thought that the director's business was not to be noticed either by the critics or the public, though I have often been impressed by directors who do obviously manipulate their actors. I remember seeing Granville-Barker's production of *The Madras House* in the twenties at the Ambassador's Theatre and being bowled over by his skill, the movement and the shape of the production, especially in the elaborate first act, though everything seemed quite spontaneous.

My greatest satisfaction as a director was in 1949 when I was asked, at the eleventh hour, to direct *The Heiress*. I was acting in a play called *The Return of the Prodigal* at the Globe Theatre with Sybil Thorndike and was preparing to act in and direct Fry's play, *The Lady's Not for Burning*. Oliver Messel, who was to design it, arranged to show me the model for the set. We had been discussing it for nearly a year and I was very excited to see it. Beaumont and I drove down to Messel's studio one evening after my performance and he suddenly said to me: 'There's a terrible crisis about *The Heiress* – we've had to get rid of the director. Could you take over?' And I said, 'When is it to open?' And he replied 'Monday week'.

Luckily, I had seen the play in America about six months before, with Wendy Hiller and Basil Rathbone, and liked it very much, so I knew what it was about. I told Beaumont I would do my best.

I enquired about the scenery and Beaumont told me it was being built in a carpenter's shop in Waterloo. I went down and examined the set carefully in the morning before I met the company. At the theatre I found James Donald, who was playing the juvenile lead, sitting gloomily on the empty stage saying 'I've offended Sir Ralph'. Everyone, it seemed, was at daggers drawn, the play was not ready, but nobody wanted me to take over the direction, fearing that I would immediately try to rearrange everything and the result would be chaos. Even my friends in the cast had doubts about accepting me to direct the play, because I have such a reputation for changing things at every rehearsal. I do it because I believe actors have to try things and then discard them and try others. I am very restless as a director and very apt to change my mind. I expect the actors to sift the wheat from the chaff, and know when I suggest good ideas and how to discard the bad ones.

The next night, after my own performance in *The Prodigal*, we had a rehearsal and I asked to be shown one of the scenes that had already been prepared. The stage manager, the management, the casting director and the authors, Mrs Goetz and her husband who had adapted the play from Henry James' novel, *Washington Square*, collected in the auditorium and the actors began to rehearse a few scenes. They had all learned their lines, they were all very well cast. Little by little, over the next hour or so, they began to gain confidence in what I rather timidly suggested. I said a few things that were right and I suddenly realized that I had won over the confidence of the company. I found that no props had been arranged, no noises off-stage of carriages driving up, people were without muffs or fans (it was a Victorian play) — all the details had been completely neglected. So naturally, when I began to pay attention to all those things, it seemed to come together quite easily. We rehearsed about seven or eight days and opened at Brighton to an enormous success.

Directing opera is a different kind of challenge, which I have several times had the opportunity of taking up, with varying success. I did *Don Giovanni* at the opening of the Coliseum when the opera moved there from Sadler's Wells in 1968, and it was a terrible failure for which I know I was greatly to blame. The conditions with opera are very difficult. You are presented with a cast you know nothing about (unless you are a singer yourself) and you have got to learn the opera by heart from records. Before that, in 1957, I had directed *The Trojans* and spent about a year beforehand studying it and it came out reasonably well. Then I did Benjamin Britten's *A Midsummer*

Night's Dream and knowing the play so well of course was a great help. I did *The Beggar's Opera* at the Haymarket during the War with Michael Redgrave, but I tried to be too clever and do it in the Regency style. I had happened to see a statuette in Edinburgh of a Regency actor playing Macbeth and I thought we would not copy Nigel Playfair and do an eighteenth-century *Beggar's Opera*, but try a nineteenth-century approach. It was not a good idea. It changed the colour of the play and gave it a Dickensian atmosphere.

I was greatly helped in *The Trojans* by Sir David Webster, who was a great friend of mine and saw me through all the hard times with the chorus, which numbered no less than 120. We rehearsed for an extra week in Chenies Street and I was bewildered by the volume of noise. I did not know how to stop them, and when I succeeded at last, could not get them started again. They all seemed to do knitting in their half-hour breaks. However, I was very fortunate because for the first production of *The Trojans* I had Blanche Thebom from America and for the second Kirsten Meyer, both of whom played Dido beautifully and were excellent actresses as well, which solved a lot of my problems. Miss Thebom was nevertheless rather autocratic about her clothes. I was sitting next to the designer, Mariano Andreu, on the first night and he said, 'My God, she's cut off half her train.' And then she came on in a wonderful gold peplum which he had designed for her big aria in the last act, and she had put a belt round it to show off her beautiful figure. One of the things that amazed me was that singers never seemed to wait for notes. We would have a dress rehearsal and they would all be gone by the time I got up to the stage at the end. They expected to have notes given by my secretary. I had no secretary, but it was some kind of etiquette in the opera world.

Of course I loved working with the music, and I was fortunate with that too, because Rafael Kubelik conducted *The Trojans* in the first year and Georg Solti in the second, and they both seemed very sympathetic to my efforts. I quickly came to realize that the moment the conductor comes onto the scene, he really is the boss. The chorus master is an important overseer too, and liable at any moment to cancel all one's carefully prepared groupings by insisting that certain voices must be in the place demanded to achieve a proper balance of the music, and with a direct view of the conductor's baton. I did find it very bewildering when I had arranged this huge chorus of 120 in groups that I thought were quite effective with ups and downs, to suit their heights and sizes, and then suddenly the chorus master would say 'You can't have your tenor there, the tenors have to be all together on this side' or 'the altos have to be somewhere else.' For rehearsals at Covent Garden they have a long bridge, with only a rail on one side of it, that crosses the orchestra pit, which is very wide. I used to run from the very back of the auditorium, tear up the ladder leading to the rickety bridge onto the stage, seize a lady in the chorus round the waist and move her from one group to another, and she would go on singing and not take the slightest notice. If you tried to explain the scenes they did not seem to find it very interesting. So you had to do a lot of coaxing and try to remember their names and take trouble not to treat them like a lot of cattle.

I have, of course, used music in many of my stage productions. We had very pretty music in *Much Ado* and also in *The School for Scandal*. It is a pity we do not have live orchestras any more. In the old days, if the play was not very successful or was rather thin such orchestral interludes brightened things up a little, although it was often somewhat grim, with an awful chamber orchestra sawing away under a lot of imitation palm leaves, playing tea-shop music between the acts.

One of the innovations that is not so successful, though I do not really understand why, is taped sound effects. In *Noah* all the noises of wild animals and birds were performed by the actors in the wings and it was splendid. I have never seen the storm in *Lear* really properly done, though with recorded sound one might expect something spectacularly effective, and yet controlled.

One of my great satisfactions in the war years was to persuade William Walton to do the music for *Macbeth*. Naturally it had to be done on records. Walton came to the first rehearsal when I was trying to do the scene with the witches, getting them to emphasize the rhythm in the doggerel they have to speak. He listened to this rehearsal for only half an hour and went away. Four weeks later, when we were finishing rehearsals, I was told that the music was ready and could be recorded. I thought it was extraordinary and feared it would not fit properly, so I went up to the big recording studio in Maida Vale and there was a huge orchestra, about fifty pieces. I found that all the witches' scenes had been perfectly timed, exactly to the rhythm of the words, just as I had sketched them out. It took many hours to record—far too long—and, with three hours extra time to pay for, I found myself signing cheques like Ludwig of

Bavaria. However, the music was most effective and we took it on tour and used it afterwards for six months in London. I was not so pleased, however, to hear it again some years later, in a production of Thornton Wilder's *The Skin of our Teeth*. As the records belonged to the management, Beaumont had decided to make use of them again.

CHAPTER
SEVEN

1955–1978

The past two decades have brought me two rewarding new forms of acting. I found, somewhat to my surprise, that I enjoyed working in films; and I had several parts in exciting modern plays, very different from anything I had done before.

I had tended to avoid making films. In the days of the silent film and the early talkies, I made *The Good Companions* with Victor Saville in 1931, and *The Secret Agent* with Alfred Hitchcock in 1935, but since I was always acting in the theatre at night, I found filming terribly exhausting. I had to get up very early in the morning and was always fidgeting to get away by five or six for the evening performance, so I grew to dislike working for the cinema. Of course, I was paid more money than in the theatre, but I had a feeling that no one thought I was sufficiently good-looking to be very successful. I was happy working with stars like Jessie Matthews and Madeleine Carroll, who were both delightful, but the directors were naturally inclined to give them the best advantage of the camera, while I was seen mostly from the back of my head—which fortunately had some hair on it in those days. In *The Secret Agent* I played with Peter Lorre, the very striking German actor who played 'M' for Fritz Lang. He was a morphine addict and an expert in stealing scenes by putting in extra unrehearsed business at the take. Lilli Palmer made her first appearance in *The Secret Agent*, in just one scene. I enjoyed working with Hitchcock, he was a great joker, but I did not have much

Spooner in *No Man's Land,* directed by Peter Hall, National, 1975

With Peter Lorre in *The Secret Agent*, directed by Alfred Hitchcock, 1935. 'Lorre was a morphine addict and an expert in stealing scenes by putting in extra unrehearsed business at the take'

Cassius in *Julius Caesar*, Hollywood, 1952, directed by Joseph Mankiewicz

The one-armed Lord Raglan in *The Charge of the Light Brigade*, 1967, directed by Tony Richardson

Left: Inigo Jollifant in the film of J. B. Priestley's *The Good Companions*, with Jessie Matthews confidence in my talent as a film actor and I thought when I saw the film that I was rather poor. In the three or four silent films I made I knew I had been perfectly ridiculous, over-acting grotesquely.

Joseph Mankiewicz's *Julius Caesar*, made in 1952, was the first film I really enjoyed making. The producers wanted to emphasize the political side of the play and Caesar was played as a Tammany boss, so it was said, though I did not see much sign of it. One or two effective scenes in the play were left out, such as the 'Cinna the poet' scene and the scene when Portia sends the boy to the Senate House, but the film was made with sincerity and was quite well mounted, except for the battle scenes, which were done in a great hurry in the Hollywood Bowl on the last day of shooting, when I was nearly killed by a horse leaping on top of me. The set for Caesar's house appeared to be so full of gongs and statues and elephants' tusks that you could hardly move, so I plucked up my courage and said to Mankiewicz: 'I don't think Roman rooms were quite so full of clutter as this,' and he had a lot of it taken away. The big set for the opening scene had been built for *Ben Hur* in Italy and then transferred to Hollywood and re-erected. But when I took a very erudite friend to see the Forum set one day he remarked 'This is quite good, but all the statues are of Emperors who haven't been born yet.'

Brutus was played by James Mason and I very much enjoyed working with him and thought his performance under-rated by the critics, since Brutus is certainly the most difficult part in the play. He was extremely kind and generous to me. I was the only Englishman out there (of course Mason was English too but he had not been in England for a long time) and I was afraid the Americans would think I was the star actor from London who had come over to teach them how to play Shakespeare. So I kept my mouth shut as much as possible and we all got on very well together. I got the part of Cassius almost by accident. Mankiewicz had come to London to get Paul Scofield to play Mark Antony. He saw me as Benedick (Paul was playing Don Pedro in my production) and engaged me for Cassius. But when Brando's tests for Antony arrived they were so successful that he was engaged and Scofield never even made the test.

I was amused to find that the huge crowd of extras were all paid different salaries. The ones in the front row who had the most striking faces were the highest paid, next came those who were only vaguely seen, and the ones at the back of the crowd who were not seen at all were the lowest paid but were able to keep their trousers on under

192

their togas. One of my favourite moments was when a whole menagerie of animals, sheep, dogs and pigeons, was brought in to make the streets of Rome look more lively. The pigeons were put on the statues and plinths and I could not understand why they did not fly away. I was told later that their wings were clipped. Next day, I was waiting to go on the set when one of the pigeons, which had been perched on a pillar, jumped off and began walking about on the floor of the studio. A hefty cowboy, who evidently looked after all the animals, dashed up and yelled at the bird, 'Get back, get back, don't you want to work tomorrow?' I was told by a friend who acted in a film with Lassie, the star dog, that every day they used to bring an entire wagonful of Lassies to the studio: the smiling Lassie, the scowling Lassie, the gloomy Lassie and so on, and there was a great argument when she won an Academy prize as to which Lassie should appear at the dinner to collect the coveted award.

I was surprised to find that I did not have to alter my stage performance for the film to any great extent, and my knowledge of the play was a great help. Marlon Brando, on the other hand, was greatly hampered by the fact that he did not know how the scenes were placed by Shakespeare or how they progressed from one climax to another. They would photograph him for a couple of days in the taxing speeches of the Forum scene, and then he would lose his voice and be unable to work. They would fill in time by filming the extras, taking a lot of shots of faces in the crowd responding, then Brando would recover and come down to the studio to do another speech. I imagine that the director hoped he could put it all together in the cutting-room, but Shakespeare is too big for that.

Brando was very self-conscious and modest, it seemed to me. He would come on to the set in his fine, tomato-coloured toga, his hair cropped in a straight fringe, and would look around nervously, expecting to find someone making fun of his appearance. Then he would take out a cigarette and stick it behind his ear. He told me that he was so well-off that he sent all his money home to his father and that he really had no need to work at all. I begged him to play Hamlet, and said that I would like to direct him if he did, but he said he never wanted to go back to the theatre.

I had only one scene with him in the film. We went through the speeches in the morning and he asked me 'What did you think of the way I did those speeches?' So I went through them with him and made some suggestions. He thanked me very politely and went away. The next morning, when we shot the scene, I found that he had taken note of everything I had said and spoke the lines exactly as I had suggested.

The next time I came down to shoot, Mankiewicz said 'Oh Marlon's done the great speech over the body absolutely marvellously,' and asked me to see the rushes, which I did not like very much. I thought he was giving a bad imitation of Olivier, but it was hardly my place to say so. I never met Brando again, which was a pity because I felt that he was enormously responsive. The very first day I was introduced to him he said, 'You must come and do a speech for me—one of my Antony speeches. I've got a tape recorder in my dressing-room.' He had tapes of Maurice Evans and John Barrymore and three or four other actors and listened to them every day to improve his diction. I thought he would have made a wonderful Oedipus.

After *Caesar*, I had no film offers until I did Clarence for Olivier in *Richard III*, which involved only a few short scenes. Then Tony Richardson asked me to go to Hollywood to play in *The Loved One* from the Evelyn Waugh novel. We became good friends at once, and in 1967 he asked me to play Lord Raglan in *The Charge of the Light Brigade*, a most amusingly written part.

We went to Turkey for twelve weeks with a huge cast and lived most of the time in a hotel in Ankara, driving out to the Crimean plains at half past five every morning, with marvellous spreads of food under canvas twice a day. I cannot think how it was done. A charming actor called Mark Dignam was with me in most of my scenes and we spent weeks in terrific heat, sitting on horseback side by side. I dread horses and cannot ride at all, and since I had to have one arm tucked inside my overcoat—Lord Raglan lost one in the Battle of Waterloo—balancing on horseback was rather difficult. The first time I went for a riding lesson in Turkey, the horse just threw me off, lay down and kicked its legs in the air. I had to remount the wretched animal at once and pretend I loved it. I was terrified that the horse would bolt and I would not know how to stop it. There was one scene involving an enormous procession of horses and marching troops. Hundreds of actors assembled on the top of a ridge and I was right out in front with two men on each side of my horse to prevent it from suddenly bolting. There was a very long take, and I remember thinking that if the horse did decide to bolt, it would ruin the whole set-up, which had taken hours to get ready. Fortunately, the animal behaved rather well.

The principal players were each supposed to have individual horses. However, soldiers from the Turkish Army were also being employed and when we were not there they would borrow the horses to ride themselves, so that when we got them back, they did not know us any more. The Turks were very tough with us, did not care for us at all and made things as difficult as they could for Tony Richardson.

I am, I suppose, lucky in that the physical discomforts of filming do not worry me unduly. I am no longer troubled by getting up early, sitting about for hours, and coping with the make-up and continuity departments, which can be tedious and exhausting. I find now that I am rather good at quietly doing my crossword and watching other people's scenes. One does, after all, have plenty of spare time to think about one's part, gossip with one's colleagues and have fun. The routine and discipline of filming are quite different from those of the theatre—occasionally one even has an evening off, and one lives more luxuriously, unless the location is particularly difficult. In the theatre you can digest a scene over two or three weeks of rehearsal and experiment; in films you only rehearse five or six times before the scene is shot. It is no good being hysterical or highly-strung in movies. At the same time you have got to have all the energy ready coiled up inside you.

There are drawbacks of course. It is usually fearfully hot under the lights; a tight or uncomfortable costume can be very tiring to wear all day. The severest torture in film-making, however, is dubbing, which I really hate. Nowadays it is used a great deal, especially with films made abroad. You have to go into a horrid little room and see yourself fifty times over, saying the same line or two with a guide strip going over your face to tell you exactly the moment to speak. You think 'Oh, I'll say that line better now, I'm sure,' but you cannot, because if you change it it does not match your lip movements, so you end by giving, with great difficulty, a cold-blooded imitation of something you did more or less spontaneously the first time.

By far the most exciting film I have ever made was Alain Resnais' *Providence*. I was very impressed by David Mercer's script. My own part was fascinating, if somewhat alarming; a very tough, Augustus John kind of character, drunk half the time, lying in bed drinking white wine and throwing bottles about, and roaring a lot of very coarse dialogue. He is an old man trying to finish a novel and at the same time dying of cancer and confusing the novel with his own past

Clive Langham in *Providence*, 1976, directed by Alain Resnais, with Ellen Burstyn, Dirk Bogarde, and David Warner. 'I felt I was in the *avant-garde* with a vengeance'. Below: With Alain Resnais, director of *Providence*; 'Resnais seemed to have great confidence in me and I threw myself into the work, acting scenes that would have embarrassed me dreadfully to do on stage'

life. His wife has killed herself by cutting her wrists in a bath and he feels he may have been responsible. He has never got on well with his son and daughter-in-law. He keeps inventing scenes for the novel which involve them in various situations, settings and contexts. He has curious nightmares about werewolves and people being hunted in forests and herded into stadiums. Finally in the last part of the film, there is a beautiful scene on the old man's seventy-eighth birthday, when he gives a lunch party in his garden for his family. His son arrives with his wife, and his illegitimate son too, and they all get on very well, drink his health and leave him with the empty garden in the sunshine. A touching end to a somewhat macabre story.

The whole structure of the film was rather oblique and as it came at the same time as I was playing Pinter's *No Man's Land*, I felt I was in the *avant-garde* with a vengeance. The director, Alain Resnais, had never done a film with English dialogue before, except for *Stavisky* which he made in America. He does not speak English very well, but he is married to the daughter of the late André Malraux, who speaks perfect English and is always there, working at his side—a delightful woman. I took an enormous liking to Resnais the moment I met him and he seemed to like me too.[1]

The part seemed to have wonderful opportunities, though I was afraid that I would not be sufficiently craggy for it. However, Resnais seemed to have confidence in me, and I threw myself into the work, acting scenes that would have embarrassed me dreadfully on the stage. At one point I was asked to put suppositories up my bottom under the bedclothes and play a scene in the lavatory which I confess I found somewhat intimate.

Resnais was wonderful to work with, so beautifully impassive, always the same whether it was fine or wet, hot or cold. We had very tricky times with the weather. We were near Limoges, in a beautiful park, where we played the last scene, with the crew in windcheaters and parka hoods, stamping their feet to keep warm, while I lay in a tropical Palm Beach suit, on a *chaise longue,* trying to pretend it was lovely weather. Resnais interrupted very little. I used to say 'Is that scene all right?' and he would say 'Well, it amused me.' I had splendid actors to work with. There were only five of us, very strongly contrasted: Dirk Bogarde, whom I have known for many years, but only worked with once before; and David Warner, Elaine Stritch and Ellen Burstyn.

It was fascinating to see how *Providence* evolved in the rushes. I remember going along to see one scene in which I did not appear. In the scene a man is being hunted down in a wood. Five men with rifles come out of the bushes and move in for the kill. I suppose I saw twelve takes of this scene, yet each time I saw it, though I knew the men were going to come out of those bushes, I became terrified as they emerged. It showed how wonderfully it was grouped and photographed.

Resnais has a genius for individual grouping. In *Marienbad* it was rather like watching a chess game – all those people in the palace gardens standing in set attitudes. In *Providence* there is a fine shot of the static scene at the lunch table, at the end of the film. A camera on an enormous crane focused on us all as we began our meal, sitting round the table with the servants, and the big dogs sitting nearby. Then the camera went up into the air over an enormous expanse of trees and sky, and did a complete semi-circle. As it slowly came down again the servants were seen clearing away the lunch. It was a most beautiful shot and took a long time both to act and to photograph. We had to keep still for abour four minutes before the camera came back to us again. Everything, every camera movement, detail, piece of furniture, was carefully thought out by Resnais beforehand.

Many people found it difficult to distinguish reality from fantasy in *Providence*. I think that, with a film of such complexity, you have to make your own judgement about what is reality and what is not. Some of the people who did not understand it in America said that the last scene, the reconciliation, should have come first, and then all the early part would have been clear. But the structure is deliberately created by Mercer and Resnais to fascinate and intrigue the audience. It makes the film almost like a thriller. You cannot think what is going to happen next when you see a man with hair on his hands being chased through a forest by riflemen. There are scenes in a law court, others in a rather chic flat, and yet more in my Victorian bedroom, with the rain pelting down outside, and the old man knocking back another drink and trying to create another scene for his novel. It is enormously varied, there is no chance of getting bored.

When I made films in the thirties I always felt that I had to be careful exactly how I looked, and this made me camera-shy. Now, when I play character parts and it does not matter how hideous I look, I lose my desire to exhibit and try to live inside the part. When I was doing *Caesar* in Hollywood I observed James Mason's technique, particularly in close-ups, and saw how brilliantly he expressed a character's thoughts without making faces or grimacing. I began to watch films with a different attitude—studying the way actors restrained their facial play so effectively.

One of the oddest films I have ever made was *The Prime Minister*, in which I played Disraeli. Possibly because I have a big nose, some people think that I have Jewish blood and am perfect for Jewish parts. I always rather hoped this was so because so many of the best actors in the world are Jewish. But I asked my father and he assured me that there is no Jewish blood in our family at all.

I have never had much luck with Jewish characters. I had no success as Shylock, though Olivier was kind enough to say it was one of the best things he had ever seen me do. I tried to play him as a little monster, shabby and dirty, with a foreign accent. However, it was in 1938 when the Nazis were in power and I think that the public in England would have preferred to see a more sympathetic, heroic Shylock, which is what they expected from me as a romantic actor.

The War was a year old when I came to play the screen Disraeli and air raids were taking place every night. The extras used to get very cross if I fluffed my lines and prevented them from getting home before the blackout. The script showed Disraeli 'from the cradle to the grave' and I had a very enterprising make-up man to create whatever age was necessary. I would play a scene in the morning as the old Disraeli, covered with fish skin (which gave me impetigo) and then they would scrape it all off so that I could do an earlier scene as the overdressed young dandy in the afternoon. The film was made on a shoestring at Teddington and, soon after, the studios were bombed and one of the managers was killed.

I had one scene in which I sat in a low chair by a fire reading through some old love-letters from my recently dead wife. I had no words to say and it was the only scene that turned out well. For the first time I realized that filming must be treated as if it were silent, and that although the dialogue must be studied and put over as it would be in the theatre, there must be more spontaneity and less emphasis. On the stage I have always had a tendency to make faces—what my intimate friends call my 'Shylock' face. I screw up my eyes and pull my mouth down and look very peculiar. I try very hard not to do that on the screen and, in watching the rushes, I am always on the look-out for unfortunate mannerisms.

Disraeli in *The Prime Minister*, 1940

Below: A gentleman's gentleman in *Murder on the Orient Express*, 1974, directed by Sidney Lumet. 'I am rather good at sitting about and doing my crossword'

I have always wanted to play the old king in *Henry IV* and when the National Theatre was about to open I implored Ralph Richardson to play Falstaff again, with me as the old King and perhaps Finney and Scofield for the younger parts but Ralph would not do it. I was therefore delighted to have the chance to play the King in Orson Welles' *Chimes at Midnight*, even though it did not turn out a great success. Like most of Orson's films it was full of very fascinating things but it did not work as a whole, though it did have a real Shakespearian feeling.

Orson Welles was splendid to work with, although he was always pressed for money and usually in poor health.[2] He engaged a very fine company but he could not afford to keep us all permanently employed. I went over for a week's shooting in Spain, then Margaret Rutherford went over for a week, then Jeanne Moreau, and Orson, who was playing Falstaff, had still not done any of his own scenes. By the time he got round to them he was tired out and there was nobody left for him to act with. I never even saw him made up as Falstaff until I watched the film in the cinema. He had found a marvellous setting for the court scenes, a great empty building in the hills above Barcelona, which had been a prison at one time and had a huge hall with a stone floor. However there was no glass in the windows and the cold November air poured in. I was wearing tights and a dressing gown and practically nothing else for my death scene. I would sit on my throne with a tiny electric fire to warm my feet while Orson spent his last pesetas sending out to buy brandy to keep me going.

I had first met Orson with the Oliviers. We were due to stay with them in the country and went down with them in their car. Orson sat in front and I leaned forward and said, 'What are you doing here?'

'I'm going to play Othello.'

'On the stage—in London?' I asked with rather tactless incredulity and he was not at all pleased. Next day we all got up rather early but Orson had already disappeared. He left word that he had a business appointment in London and I thought perhaps he had been very offended by me. At about nine o'clock that night the bell suddenly rang and he came in. The servants had gone to bed and Vivien Leigh went off and made scrambled eggs for him in the kitchen. I asked Orson if he had had a good day in London. 'Not at all,' he said, 'she cried the whole time.'

We once had a hilarious day making recordings of an episode of a Sherlock Holmes series for the radio. I was Sherlock Holmes, Ralph

Richardson was Dr Watson and Orson came over to play Moriarty. We all went to lunch at the Étoile in Charlotte Street and Orson shouted and drew so much attention to us that everyone in the restaurant began staring. Ralph and I felt like two little boys from Eton who had been taken out at half-term by a benevolent uncle.

I have always wanted to make a film of *The Tempest*. Prospero has been a favourite part of mine and it would be a wonderful thing to do at the end of one's career, because it is so obviously Shakespeare's last work—the end of his career.

My first Prospero was in 1930 at the Old Vic with Harcourt Williams. Leslie French was very charming as Ariel, singing beautifully, and naked except for a loin-cloth. It was seeing his performance that is supposed to have inspired Eric Gill to create the statue in the front of Broadcasting House.

In all four productions of the play I have acted in over the years, with Harcourt Williams, George Devine, Peter Brook and Peter Hall, I was consistent in one thing—I never looked at Ariel. He was always behind me or above me, never in front of me. I tried to see him in my mind's eye, never looking at him physically. It heightened the impression of Ariel as a spirit.

In directing the play in 1957 for Stratford, and afterwards for Drury Lane, Peter Brook conceived the last scene in the play as the great triumph for Prospero returning home to accept the dukedom; I had a beautiful blue robe with a coronet which I placed on my head as Ariel dressed me. At the end, as I moved to the back of the stage, some ropes fell from above, the other characters turned their backs to the audience and the scene changed and became a ship sailing away, then I turned and came down to the front to speak the Epilogue. But in 1974 Peter Hall wanted me to play Prospero as a disillusioned man who had kept his old court suit in his cave for twenty years and got it out very reluctantly. He felt that Prospero did not want his dukedom back and resented having to leave his island. My reading of the Epilogue thus became quite different, more humble and not as grandiloquent as in the Peter Brook version.

Komisarjevsky, curiously enough, told me back in the twenties that I ought to play Prospero without a beard. He said, 'You ought to

Right: Orson Welles directing *Chimes at Midnight*, 1964. 'By the time he got round to his own scenes he was tired out and there was nobody left for him to act with'.
Below: As King Henry IV in *Chimes at Midnight*, with Keith Baxter as Prince Hal

look like Dante!' and that is how I tried to look in the Vic production, clean shaven, with a turban. Peter Hall, in contrast, insisted on my putting on a pointed grey beard. He wanted me to look like the Elizabethan wizard Doctor John Dee, and he and John Bury designed a costume and make-up with which I was never very happy. In Peter Brook's production I had invented my own costume with his help, and tried to look like a figure from an El Greco painting, half naked above the waist and wearing sandals to give me the look of a hermit. At the Vic, in 1940, when George Devine directed me in the play, I had a small grey beard and spectacles. It was interesting playing the part in these different ways and I found effective things in all of them.

Caliban is always a difficult part to cast in *The Tempest*. He must be a tragic figure as well as providing comic relief. In 1930, Ralph Richardson contrived to combine both these qualities to perfection I remember seeing one production with an actor called Louis Calvert, who wore an animal skin and walked about on all fours like a pantomime bear and was perfectly ridiculous. Benson used to play Caliban hanging from a tree, eating a fish, while Tree arranged a final tableau for the end of the play, with Caliban stretched out on a headland, lonely and forlorn, and a model ship moving away in the distance.

The first time I ever appeared in the play, as a very young man, I was asked to play Ferdinand for a few matinées with an actor called Henry Baynton who was starring as Caliban. The scenery, with a lot of potted palms, was old and dreadful and the cast was dressed in terrible hired clothes and wigs. Baynton prefaced his entrance with tremendous roars offstage and then emerged from a cave in the centre of the stage in a splendid, specially designed costume. He was an extraordinary performer who would play Caliban one night and Hamlet the next. At the end of *Lear* he would whip off his make-up and come on in a smart dressing gown to take the calls. He played Hamlet with a string of pearls round his neck, which I thought was going rather too far.

I think *The Tempest* would make a wonderful film and have my own ideas about how it could be done. The play has to be set in several, unidentifiable, locations: marshes one minute, cornfields the next, then cliffs and sea, and finally sands. Japan would be marvellous for this, remembering the beautiful effects of *Rashomon*. I once asked Benjamin Britten if he would compose the music

Prospero in *The Tempest*. Left: In
Peter Hall's production at the National
1974, and (below) in Peter Brook's
production at Stratford and Drury Lane,
1957

Spooner in *No Man's Land*, by Harold Pinter. The National Theatre production directed by Peter Hall and recorded by Granada TV in 1978. 'I just had this wonderful feeling which was instinctive after I read the play; this is how the man should look'

Below: With Ralph Richardson as Hirst in *No Man's Land*, directed by Peter Hall, 1975. 'It is wonderful to play with someone who is absolutely opposite you in temperament'

for such a film and he agreed. He suggested that the earlier parts should have an ordinary soundtrack, but when the scene moved to the island there should be no noises, only music.

In recent years I have found myself appearing more and more in modern plays, notably Alan Bennett's *40 Years On,* Edward Bond's *Bingo,* Charles Wood's *Veterans,* David Storey's *Home* and Harold Pinter's *No Man's Land.* I am proud and thrilled to feel that in the latter two plays I have had not only a personal success but also a wonderful partnership with Ralph Richardson.

I read *No Man's Land* in forty minutes and knew instantly that I must play the part of Spooner. Peter Hall had sent the script to me expecting that I would want to play the 'posh' part of Hirst, because it was more the kind of role I had done in the past. I told him 'Don't be silly. The other part is infinitely more what I want to play.' The part of Spooner was a complete impersonation, such as I had never had a chance to do in the theatre. It was very exciting to have a chance of doing it, and I was quick in finding a way to look and to dress. The moment I read the play I saw Spooner clearly, which was rare for me. I remember saying to Harold Pinter 'I think Auden, don't you? Do you think sandals and socks?' and he jumped at the idea. Then I said 'Do you think we should add spectacles?' and he liked that too. About a week after we started rehearsal I came on the stage with the wig, the suit and the spectacles and everybody said 'It's exactly right, perfect!' And I said 'Yes, and now I must find a performance to go inside it!'

It took longer to find a voice for Spooner. I did not want anything too affected. I eventually found it by throwing back to my eldest brother's generation. I had a very brilliant brother, Lewis, who was something of a poet. He was badly wounded in the First War, and lived abroad most of his life. When I was a boy I visited him once or twice at Oxford—he was at Magdalen after the First War. He was a great friend of Aldous Huxley, the Haldanes and all the intellectual Oxford people who afterwards joined the Bloomsbury Group. Many of them had a curious drawl which I remembered vividly, and I adopted it for Spooner. I also had in mind the bookshops in the Charing Cross Road where I used to buy cutouts of the ballet. They were run by Bohemian semi-failures who were very much the kind of man Spooner seemed to be.

One reason I so enjoy working with Ralph Richardson is that we are old friends and we laugh a lot and seem to balance each other's style in a very happy way. It is wonderful to play with somebody who is so absolutely opposed to you in temperament: we are a tremendous contrast in personality. Now, after so many performances and interviews together, we say we are becoming like the broker's men in *Cinderella*. People even mix us up and greet us by each other's names, particularly in America where titles often confuse the public. When we first read the plays neither of us was quite sure whether we dared to undertake them, fearing we might make fools of ourselves, but we were very fortunate in our directors, Lindsay Anderson and Peter Hall. Both of them had enormous feeling for the plays and we felt they would not have wanted us to play in them unless they were confident that we were the right men for the parts. There was no question of being engaged because we were stars, as sometimes is the case in more commercial plays.

In *No Man's Land* lots of people came round after every performance, both in London and America, complaining that they did not understand the play. 'What does it mean?' they would ask. Why should the play 'mean' anything if the audience was held the whole time and was never bored? That is surely the important thing. I do not think *No Man's Land* has any deep social significance. Pinter is a marvellous writer of character and suspense and, although people tried to make out that the play was about God, the decline of England or any number of other symbolic things, it was enough for me that the audience was fascinated and mystified. Certainly a few people walked out, but that is true of any play, and the general appreciation of it both here and in America was extraordinary.

Unhappily George Devine had died by the time Ralph and I did *Home* at the Royal Court. Irving Wardle has written a splendid book about him – one of the best stage biographies I have ever read. He interviewed me while he was writing it and I felt as we talked that I had been ungenerous to George. All the people who worked with him at the Court, like Tony Richardson, Anthony Page and Peggy Ashcroft, were devoted to him. He and I had rather an awkward relationship because I had known him from the very beginning when he was my undergraduate Mercutio at Oxford. Then he was with me for a number of years in my seasons in the 1930s and was excellent in

Left: The Headmaster in *40 Years On*,
by Alan Bennett, Apollo 1968

Right: Shakespeare in
Edward Bond's *Bingo*,
directed by Jane Howell,
Royal Court, 1974

With Ralph Richardson in David Storey's *Home*,
directed by Lindsay Anderson, Royal Court, 1970

many small but difficult parts. He went to India to fight in the war and came back to take over at the Court in the 1950s. He and I directed *Lear* together in 1955, the Noguchi *Lear* in London, which was rather a disaster. He had become tremendously fond of Michel St-Denis and had been one of the founders of his schools at Islington and the Old Vic with Glen Byam Shaw. I suppose I felt slightly jealous because he and Glen (and the Motleys) had been with me so long, and then left me to work with Michel. Devine did once ask me to play at the Court in Beckett's *Endgame*, which I did not like at all (he played it himself afterwards) and he also asked me to be in John Osborne's *A Patriot For Me*, in a part which I did not care for. I did not see much of him in his last years. I am very sorry now; I am sure I missed a lot by not allowing him to influence me in his enthusiasm for new writers of the *avant-garde*, but he and Michel were always tremendously taken with Brecht and Beckett, with neither of whom I have been able to find much sympathy.

One of the hardest things I ever tackled was to direct myself and perform solo in the Shakespeare recital, *Ages of Man*, which I toured for many years. When I opened in New York I nearly missed the first night as a result of going to Havana for a weekend just before Christmas. The hotel where I stayed seemed curiously empty and the next day the revolution broke out. I spent the whole day in the American Consul's office trying to get a visa back to New York, and I arrived back only a few hours before I was due to open. On top of that, there had been a newspaper strike in America and I was the first actor to get a notice for six weeks.

The only time the *Ages of Man* recital was not a success was when Beaumont suggested that, since I had had such success in the provinces before the War, I should take it to Edinburgh, Liverpool, Cambridge and Brighton. At Liverpool no-one would come near it and Edinburgh was very hard. In Brighton it was so badly attended for the first three nights that Alan Melville and Godfrey Winn both wrote letters to the *Sussex Gazette* and said it was an outrage that it was not a success. The theatre was packed for the rest of the week. I had to write to thank them, which I found somewhat humiliating. The audience seemed to be suspicious of a one-man show, perhaps because they felt they would not get their money's worth. I toured

Ages of Man for so many years that I feared I would be out of practice when it came to acting again with other people. Also, eight performances a week all by myself, and sitting alone in a dressing-room between the acts, was a very lonely and sometimes depressing business.

I shall, if I am lucky, continue to work in films and television but, although one can experience a wonderful stillness and a feeling of suspense in the movies, the theatre is the real sounding-board. The sensation of an audience suddenly concentrating, with not a murmur in the auditorium, is a great moment. It is very thrilling in a new play or a new part when you get that feeling for the first time, knowing that you are holding the audience completely, in total command of the battlefield.

CHAPTER
EIGHT

AMERICA

I have always looked on New York as something of a second home. I have been unusually lucky in my work here, and have made many friends both in the theatre and outside it. I have watched the city grow and change ever since my first sight of it all those years ago, in 1928, and looked forward ever since to the many opportunities of returning here. To me, Fifth Avenue, from St. Patrick's Cathedral to the Plaza, is one of the finest and most elegant streets in the world, and the towers of Central Park West, twinkling with their myriad lights as dusk begins to fall, are for me among the most magical and romantic sights imaginable. Even the extremes of climate, the crumbling pavements, insistent traffic, the extraordinary mixture of luxury and squalor – all these contrasting elements never fail to absorb and excite me. I work well, eat and sleep well and look forward with liveliest expectation to whatever the following day may chance to bring.

I am surprised to find, in looking back, how many times I have acted and directed in New York. The *Hamlet* production of 1936 was of course my first and most important experience in this country, and how lucky I was to be presented by the McClintic-Katharine Cornell management with such distinguished colleagues as Judith Anderson and Lillian Gish, two wonderful actresses who took me under their wing and were so quickly to become such lifelong friends. The enthusiastic reception of two of my own productions,

215

In the gardens at Stourhead, from the
Thames TV series *The English Garden*, 1980

The Importance of Being Earnest and, later, *The Lady's Not for Burning*, both of which had been very popular in London, gave me my next great satisfaction. But I also very much enjoyed directing *Five Finger Exercise*, Peter Shaffer's earliest success as a playwright, with its English cast, and later my friend Hugh Wheeler's play *Big Fish, Little Fish*, when for the first time I directed an all American company and greatly appreciated the chance to work with Jason Robards, Hume Cronyn, George Grizzard, Martin Gabel and Ruth White, the last a brilliant actress whose early death soon afterwards saddened me very much.

Tiny Alice was a fascinating experience, though I was always apprehensive of the difficult last act, and could not help feeling (in spite of Edward Albee's reassurance that he thought of all the characters as being about fifty) that the part of the unfrocked priest could have been more suitably played by a younger man. The previews, at which the reception of the audiences seemed excitingly mixed, were more rewarding on the whole than the later performances as far as I was concerned. Of course I loved acting again with Irene Worth; we had played together several times in England, where she was always very successful and is now so greatly missed.[1] She is a great artist as well as one of my most devoted friends. In *All Over*, which Albee generously invited me to direct, we were again encouraged by enthusiastic previews, but the critics and public failed to be interested in the play, despite the fine performances of Jessica Tandy, Colleen Dewhurst and Hume Cronyn.

I had always had a secret longing to work in the musical field, having achieved some success with two grand operas, Berlioz' *The Trojans* and Britten's *Midsummer Night's Dream*, which I had directed in London at Covent Garden, so I agreed with some excitement to an offer to direct the musical *Irene* with Debbie Reynolds. This was a grave mistake on my part, and I was finally replaced (very wisely for the production as it turned out) by Gower Champion, after a very unhappy period of rehearsals and six weeks of arguments and disagreements on the road. Although the show was an enormous success from the opening night in Toronto, no one seemed satisfied with the production. During the early rehearsals I had very stupidly informed the company that I had no experience of directing a musical and expected them to help me in my work, thus revealing a lack of authority which did little to encourage their confidence in

Tiny Alice by Edward Albee, with John Gielgud and Irene Worth, Billy Rose Theatre, New York, 1965

Richard Burton in *Hamlet,* directed by myself, at the Lunt-Fontanne Theatre, New York, 1964. The run of 136 performances broke the Broadway record for *Hamlet,* previously set by my own performance in 1936–7 my abilities. I was dismayed to find that I was supposed to rehearse the 'book' scenes but not expected to interfere with the songs and dances. These were rehearsed separately and completed without me in different studios and I found it hard to persuade the actors to work when they were tired by the rest of their exacting rehearsals. In the end, I was relieved to be free of my assignment, although I found it a somewhat shattering experience to be sacked for the first time in my long career. I realized too late that it is only the great choreographers – Champion, Jerome Robbins, Michael Bennett, Bob Fosse – who have the expertise needed to solve the complicated problems with which the American musical at its best can achieve such brilliant results.

My six months acting in the New York *Hamlet* will always remain a memorable time for me. Although the long run was an emotional strain, I was still young enough to enjoy the generosity of the company, the enthusiasm of the audiences and the chance to meet a number of important New York personalities at parties and celebrations. Of course everything has changed on Broadway since then. When our production of *Hamlet* was moving to another theatre, and I was packing my things, someone came in with a great tray with champagne and glasses. Helen Hayes, who was playing in *Victoria Regina* across the street, had sent it with the message that she was very sorry we were moving on, such a charming, courteous thing to do.[2]

In McClintic's production I managed to beat the record John Barrymore had established when he played *Hamlet* on Broadway. But it was rather ironic that in the *Hamlet* production which I directed ten years ago, Richard Burton managed to beat my record as well as Barrymore's by playing more than one hundred performances. But of this, of course, I had no idea when I received a wonderfully generous cable from Barrymore (who was ending his career somewhat tragically in Hollywood during the thirties), congratulating me on my success and telling me how amusing and complicated the part of Hamlet was and how delighted he was that I had made a success of it. I had seen his Hamlet in London in 1926 and thought him splendid, though he was already forty-five years old. Afterwards, however, when he was the guest of honour at some dinner I attended, I was shocked to see how terribly ravaged he looked, with pouches under his eyes. It was said he had to be woken up with black coffee and dragged to the theatre just in time to appear, and that he would fly into rages and attack the unfortunate young actor who played Laertes in the duelling scene so furiously that he had to be replaced every few weeks. One night he threw Fay Compton (who was playing Ophelia) to the ground during the Nunnery Scene, and when she protested later at such ungallant behaviour, he apologized and said, 'I just couldn't bear your looking so Goddam pure, with those tears running down your cheeks like rain falling on little rosy apples!'

One Sunday night, I had an invitation from Alexander Woollcott, who had been to one of our rehearsals, and had afterwards given a very enthusiastic radio talk about my performance, which helped to make the production a success. He asked me to dinner in a private room at a restaurant, and I stupidly misread the invitation and was three quarters of an hour late. When I arrived I found the whole party waiting for me – Alexander Woollcott, Thornton Wilder, Ruth Gordon and Lillian Gish. Woollcott was famous for his rages if people were unpunctual, and the others were trembling at how he would behave when I finally arrived. However, I was so plainly remorseful that he forgave me and we had a fascinating dinner. Thornton Wilder was very quiet until suddenly, towards the end of the meal, he burst like a soda-water siphon with enormous volubility. Afterwards I asked him why he had been so reserved at first and he said Woollcott had warned them to let me do all the talking because of the article he was proposing to write about me. This was not so difficult, of course, because I always talk too much.

Woollcott was said to be often venomous and unpredictable but he was always very kind to me. The last time I saw him was in 1942 when he came to London just before he died. He invited me to breakfast (which seems to be a favourite custom in America although never a favourite time for me), and sat enthroned in his suite at the Dorchester Hotel in his pajamas. When I said I was planning to do *Macbeth*, Woollcott told me that the Lunts had always wanted to produce the play.[3] 'Lynn has a wonderful idea,' he said. 'She will go naked to murder Duncan.' I agreed this would be a sensational effect, but how did she propose to do it? 'Oh,' said Woollcott, 'there will be a very high parapet between her and the audience; she will keep her pudenda strictly for Alfred.'

The Lunts were always adored by their companies, although they

were immensely exacting and never satisfied either with their own performances or anybody else's (but they were wonderfully appreciative as an audience). I have heard that Alfred Lunt, with only two nights left at the end of a long run, once called everybody back for a rehearsal. And he was continually thinking of new ways to refine and improve his own performance. In *The Visit* he invented some business at rehearsal of shaking pebbles out of his shoe—he had picked two up in Central Park that afternoon—and then said anxiously to Peter Brook, who was directing the play, 'Do you think it might be better if perhaps there were only one?' I don't think the Lunts ever stopped thinking about the theatre from the moment they woke up in the morning till the moment they went to bed at night. They probably rehearsed in bed as well. I implored them a number of years ago to make some records—a few scenes from their great successes should surely have been preserved to show something of the incomparable technique of their long and brilliant partnership. But, alas, they would never agree.

Modern American actors seem to rely very much on motivation, and certainly in their indigenous plays they practise it with admirable results. Directors of the new school demand improvisation at the early rehearsals, and games and exercises to break down self-consciousness and encourage unselfish teamwork. It is true that sitting around a table reading the text for several days—as Shaw and Granville-Barker insisted upon—can involve boredom for the cast, and personally I long for them to begin to walk about and begin blocking moves and business as soon as possible. Long introductory lectures can be dangerous too, but every director must find his own best way of starting. Peter Brook, directing Seneca's *Oedipus*, would not tell us what we were to wear or what kind of scenery he planned until he had been rehearsing for six weeks. He brought tapes of Zulu war cries for us to listen to, and engaged a professor who conducted Tai-Chi lessons for twenty minutes every morning. But when I worked in three Shakespeare productions for him we most carefully discussed and examined the text. In classic plays the diction, phrasing and rhythm are just as vital as any physical and pictorial graces which may bring the scenes to life.

The minor characters in Shakespeare may seem unrewarding to the ambitious young player because they are so loosely drawn, but

221

Alfred Lunt and Lynn Fontanne in *Idiot's Delight* by Robert Sherwood, Theatre Guild production at the Shubert Theatre, New York, 1936 he must content himself in supplying the necessary support for the great leading heroes and heroines who dominate the plays.

In Restoration comedy, too, the characters are types and have very little concrete existence apart from their actual purpose in the plays. Congreve and Sheridan revelled in their beautiful English. Their audiences listened to and laughed at the kind of people who were familiar to them, and at the basic human motives, money and sex, of which the authors made such witty use.

The Victorians preferred sensational melodrama, spectacle, farce and sentimental comedy. It was Pinero (and Henry Arthur Jones, Oscar Wilde and J. M. Barrie to a lesser extent) who began to change the picture by writing realistic problem plays. These became enormously popular, until Shaw in his reviews of Archer's translations made a small but intelligent public conscious for the first time of the genius of Ibsen, with his extraordinary new technique. His work combined realism, poetry and symbolism and a construction in which the story was rooted in events that had taken place long before the actual plays began. Playwrights of today have evolved completely new techniques, very fascinating but often a little bewildering to old-timers like myself.

One of the strongest cards in the theatrical pack is less safe to play nowadays, because of the class labelling which has become more and more apparent over the decades which spanned the two World Wars. Though oddly enough, Pinter made splendid use of a somewhat similar device in *No Man's Land* with its two sinister henchmen, for the most part we miss the use of the famous contrasting personalities of master and servant. Prince Hal and Falstaff, Don Giovanni and Leporello, the valets and maids in the plays of Molière and Goldoni and even (with the dangerous rumblings of disintegration so soon to come) in the four great Chekhov plays. These basic relationships of the masterpieces of centuries of theatre must necessarily be gone forever. Even drawing-room comedy, on which we English prided ourselves as being such supreme exponents, ceases to divert us with tennis racquets, stiff upper lips and old school ties.

When I was young, I always felt I must know the background and motivation of any new character I was asked to play, and so when I first began to be offered parts by playwrights of the new school – after 1956 – I found the experience a fairly daunting one. In

222

Shakespeare I had learned to project, and in Chekhov to act more intimately, and I felt that Granville-Barker and Komisarjevsky had both helped me to develop some skill in interpreting these authors. Congreve, Wilde and Maugham all demanded somewhat different methods of approach, but I had seemed to achieve some success in interpreting their characters, too. But the plays of Albee, Bond, Storey and Pinter were original and strange, and I relied greatly on Lindsay Anderson and Peter Hall, who directed me so ably in some of these modern plays, though I found the playwrights themselves difficult to approach and reluctant to discuss their work if I was too eager to demand detailed explanations.

The lack of conventional construction which we had always expected – such elements as abstract implications, non-sequitur dialogue, oblique references, lack of conventional theatrical climaxes and effective entrances and curtains – all these innovations filled me with apprehension. But once I found the courage to experiment, I gradually began to be more enthusiastic and hopeful. I have always been unsympathetic to the plays of Brecht and Beckett and have found difficulty in reading them and enjoying them even as an audience. But perhaps if I were to have the courage to act a part in one of their plays, I would discover a way of tackling them that might change my mind, especially if I had a sympathetic and brilliant director.

All through my early career I was disinclined to act either for films or television, but over the last fifteen years I have learned at last to enjoy working in both those media after a considerable amount of experiment and application. Tony Richardson, who cast me as Lord Raglan in *The Charge of the Light Brigade*, was the first to give me scope in a character part on the screen. Before that, Joseph Mankiewicz and John Houseman had helped me greatly with my screen performance as Cassius in *Julius Caesar*, in which James Mason was so enormously generous and cooperative. From him, too, I began to learn something about acting in close-ups and how to make so many faces before the camera.

My first experience of television was in New York in *The Browning Version*, a play that had actually been written for me by Terence Rattigan many years before, to be done in a double bill with another, *Harlequinade*. (They have just been successfully revived in London in 1980 at the National Theatre, with Alec McCowen and

Geraldine McEwan.) Hugh Beaumont, who was my manager at the time, had been dubious about the idea of two one-act plays, since such a programme had never been very successful in the West End. Though he and I were both enthusiastic about *The Browning Version*, he refused even to show me *Harlequinade*, which was in part a skit on the Lunts (who had been recently acting in a play of Rattigan's called *O Mistress Mine*), and in part a skit on me. I had directed for the very first time a production of *Romeo and Juliet*, with the students at Oxford in 1931, in which Rattigan himself had played a very small part (one of the musicians who came to waken Juliet on her wedding morning) and my mannerisms had amused him very much. In *Harlequinade* there is a joke about the perfectionist director who is always changing the flowerpot from one side to the other, and has various other tricks and mannerisms of mine as a director, as well as some of the unusual characteristics of Alfred Lunt. But Beaumont thought the Lunts would not care to be parodied and persuaded me to turn down both plays, so Rattigan, naturally disappointed, took them to another management, and they were enthusiastically received, with Eric Portman and Mary Ellis in the leading parts.

I had always been sorry not to have created the fine part of the schoolmaster in *The Browning Version*, and when I was asked to play it for television I jumped at the opportunity, especially as the medium was new to me. The other players were Robert Stephens, Margaret Leighton and Cecil Parker, and we were directed by John Frankenheimer, who was very excitable in those days, even sitting between my legs while the cameras were running, making signs and gestures to encourage me.

Much later I did a pilot film with Alan Arkin, also in New York. He was playing the part of a taxi-driver and I was supposed to be a tipsy stockbroker. We filmed in lower Manhattan on location, then a fairly new experience for me, where they took out one side of a taxicab, while the cameraman sat right in front of us on the floor, to photograph us as we drove along. It was a very hot day and we went round and round the fishmarket, which smelt to high heaven. In the next scene I had to climb onto the roof of another taxi, still rather drunk, carrying a briefcase and umbrella and wearing a bowler hat and city suit and harangue the crowd. We were shooting in a busy street opposite a girls' school, and all the girls were hanging out of

225

Katharine Cornell as Juliet with Edith Evans as the Nurse in *Romeo and Juliet,* directed by Guthrie McClintic, Martin Beck Theatre, New York, 1934 the windows and screaming with laughter. I had never had to work in public like that before, but I was determined not to be put off and managed somehow to ignore all the interruptions. It was a very good experience to have to overcome the embarrassment of having a number of onlookers so close to one, whether on location or in the studio.

Only a few months ago I had to do a scene in an alley in the middle of a bazaar in Cairo, lying in a puddle on a filthy stone staircase for about two hours, with my throat supposedly cut and my neck made up with a great gash to look as if I had been slashed with a scimitar. Everybody who passed by kept stopping and staring, but I looked up and said as gaily as I could, 'Oh, I've just cut myself shaving.'

Now I am playing a faithful butler in a new film called *Arthur* with Dudley Moore and Liza Minnelli. It is a kind of fantasy about a boy who is a millionaire and drives about in a Rolls Royce, throwing his money about and picking up hookers. He has a faithful black chauffeur and a butler who is a sort of father figure trying to make him grow up but not quite sure how to set about it. The part has some deadpan comedy with an underlying seriousness. But my first day of shooting was something of a baptism by fire. We were called to begin work at 5 A.M. in Bergdorf Goodman's, where we played an important scene, and then moved out to the pavement of Fifth Avenue where, in front of the Plaza Hotel, we filmed for three intensely hot days with hundreds of people looking on and the traffic roaring by.

During the last year I have played a remarkable variety of different characters – an orchestra conductor in a Polish film; an Egyptian curio dealer in *Sphinx*; two clergymen (one real, the other bogus) in two adaptations for television, one from an early Agatha Christie thriller, the other from a short story by Roald Dahl; a German-Jewish scientist in *The Formula*; an Arab sheikh in *Omar Mukhtar*; a publisher in a film about the life of D. H. Lawrence, *Priest of Love*; a Cambridge professor in *Chariots of Fire*; and the head of a hospital in the coming film of *The Elephant Man*. I used not to be considered to be a particularly versatile performer, and it is gratifying after all these years to be thought of for such a variety of elderly gentlemen.

Of course one soon learns how very differently one must tackle acting in films after all my years in the live theatre. One must learn to be patient, waiting for hours between takes and set-ups (I do crossword puzzles and read novels and magazines) but at the same time one must be ready to snap into one's performance the moment one is needed, ignoring the inconsistencies of continuity. Sometimes only a look may be required, sometimes only a reaction to a speech from another character, sometimes quite a long speech or scene for a main long shot. One must concentrate on the thought behind the action and try to economise and simplify wherever possible. Of course, one knows that much will depend on the way the camera is handled, and is quite ignorant of how the scenes may finally be cut and edited.

In the old days I used to study and rehearse a great deal at home and even shout my lines aloud on country walks (to the alarm of passersby), but now I wait until the moment comes to meet the author, the director and the other players. Then I work very concentratedly with the people involved, and I think it's much the best. I was amazed when I learned that Paul Muni used to record his whole performance on tape and then play it back to himself before he ever went on the set.

I have found it something of a drawback to repeat on television parts that I have created in the live theatre. But in the *Julius Caesar* film it was very helpful to know my part of Cassius so thoroughly from having played it first on the stage, where phrasing, fluency of speech and the tempo of verse is so important and difficult to repeat in a more intimate medium.

When we filmed *No Man's Land* for television our long months of performing these plays in the theatre made it hard work both for me and for Ralph Richardson to achieve an appearance of spontaneity. We felt we were too sure of the way we had decided to speak every line and respond to every situation. In the theatre one learns to select and control one's performance, but in performing to a live audience one finds a way to repeat with extreme accuracy, but also with minute variations of timing and emphasis. In films, once you decide on your performance and have created it broadly in a key scene taken in long shot, you must be prepared to repeat it in correctly similar detail in the close-ups and two-shots which complete the photographing of the whole scene. People keep coming up, maddeningly, and saying, 'You put your hand to your haversack on this line,' or, 'You touched your tie.' You did those things not knowing you did them, so that when you are then reminded of them for a week, you suddenly become frighteningly sick of the scene; it is a boring repetition of something you would rather do in a different way each time. The continuity girl is continually at your elbow, reminding you of your exact movements and gestures when the main scene was shot, yet you may also have to move your head or hands to a slightly different angle to satisfy the lighting or the camera or feed your partner from behind the camera with lines from the scene that he or she is reacting to in close-up. Wardrobe assistants and hairdressers brush you down or spruce you up, powder and dry your face just before you start to act. A babel of conversation and argument is suddenly quelled and an unnatural deadly silence falls as the fatal three bells are rung and the clapperboard is snapped jauntily within an inch of your face. Worst of all, you know that whatever you do, once accepted by the director, is there forever. No chance to develop or improve at a subsequent performance or bring greater subtlety to bear on your original conception.

Yet the intimacy of the screen can be a very useful discipline. In the live theatre, audiences are apt to encourage one's mannerisms, and it is easy to wish to gain sympathy and applause and laughter by effective manipulation of a technique which has served one well over many years.

A contemporary of mine, a wonderful actor, has been heard to say, when offered a new part, 'Which of my five old men do you want?' Sometimes I am afraid of making the same remark myself. One must go on to the end trying to experiment and break new ground and I am very grateful to continue to have opportunities to do so.

Epilogue

People sometimes say that the theatre is not needed, that thousands
of people have never seen live theatre at all, and that it will eventually die. If this is true, I can only hope that it does not happen in my
lifetime. I do not know whether the theatre is important or not: what
art is important? Does it have to be popular to be important? Even if
it does, do we perhaps underrate the popular appeal of the theatre? I
have always thought it extraordinary that the Elizabethans could
understand Shakespeare's very elaborate plays when so many of the
ordinary people were entirely uneducated. The dynastic complications of English monarchs from Richard II to Richard III are very
involved, yet the public obviously revelled in them and knew about
all the great families and their quarrels.

But then Shakespeare is unique in his universal appeal to audiences. In Shakespeare there is sound and fury, tenderness and
lyricism, humour and philosophy; and quite a number of platitudes
as well! As Shaw pointed out, a great deal of Shakespeare (especially
some of the speeches in *Hamlet* and *As You Like It*) contains every
simple truism. But they are so wonderfully phrased that you cannot
resist quoting them, and it is hardly possible to discuss art or
philosophy without Shakespeare very often coming into it, because
of the unforgettable things that he has said and the universal types
that he has created. People can understand and recognize his
characters in any language or culture. When I played *Hamlet* in

229

India, I was amazed to find how familiar many Indians were with the plays. In America, too, I have received wonderful letters about the plays; they are tremendous students of Shakespeare. There are fine collections in most universities, particularly in the Folger Library in Washington, and there is a great tradition of Shakespeare with actors such as John Drew, the Barrymores, Edwin Booth and Richard Mansfield.

There are several Shakespearian parts that have been particularly important to me: Prospero is usually considered such a bore, but I have always found people like me in the part and even seem to like the play better when I have played it. *Lear* has also been an intensely exciting play for me. It is fortunate that these two are the only two big parts that I might still play now. I was amazingly lucky with *Hamlet*. By the time I had finished with it I did not want to read or write about it any more. I had played it many hundreds of times over fifteen years, in six different productions. Shakespeare's Richard II was for many years my favourite, perhaps because I did not play it very often – not as often as I would have liked to when I was young.

It is very difficult as one gets older to jettison all one's old performances and find a new one. It was suggested that I might play *King Lear* again, but there were several changes in proposed directors, several different kinds of theatres suggested. And then I got frightened that I wouldn't be strong enough. I haven't really got the physique for Lear; I am a tenor, not a bass. Olivier, who is also a tenor, has always agreed with me that we have both played Macbeth and Lear without bass notes. In *Othello*, on the other hand, in which I failed miserably, he achieved one of his most notable successes with the aid of intense physical and vocal preparation. Yet I have done four productions and I love playing it – I think it's the most wonderful part! My fear is that with a new director I would say, 'This is what I did before, isn't this better?' If I couldn't discover a means to do it in a new way, I would find myself falling back on my old performance. And since that would only confuse one's self and one's director, I think perhaps it's better not to risk it, but to try to find something completely new.

When it comes to speaking Shakespeare I have been very lucky, because I have always had easy breath control. Though I have never been able to sing, I have never had difficulty with speaking, except that I tend to gabble. I have often been accused of inaudibility when

Epilogue

I drop my voice, just like most other people do, at the end of lines, and in private life both friends and strangers are apt to complain that I talk too fast and am often difficult to understand. But I have a very acute musical ear for phrasing. In modern plays, if there is a line or a speech I cannot speak in the way it is written, I try to persuade the author to change it or I begin improvising until he says 'I think it's better than mine'. With writers like Edward Albee, Graham Greene, Noel Coward, Bernard Shaw, Harold Pinter or David Storey, of course, it is impossible to change the lines at all. But in the average, colloquial modern play you can make the lines your own in a certain way, and I think you often have to change the phrasing or cut when you feel you cannot make a sentence clearly valid.

I am very keen on pace, and I always think it is frightfully important to ensure the audience is not bored and that they do not fall asleep or leave the theatre. Shaw always said 'speak to the lines and with the lines but never in between the lines'.

On the other hand Edith Evans was perfectly right when she said 'You must control the audience. Never give them too much opportunity for applause and laughter and tears. Don't indulge yourself by showing off; the moment that you begin to find that you can do something well, you must control it and do it more selectively. In a farce you must play as if you have a practical joke inside you but you're not going to let anybody know you think it's funny.'

This dual life that you lead on the stage is a very subtle, complicated one—marking your effects, storing them up for the next night, trying to correct what you know is not good and trying to improve on the night before, feeling when the audience encourages you to make some new point, and making yourself so free and familiar with the text that you can do exactly what you want with it without destroying its basic shape for your fellow actors or the original scheme of the director.

When I first worked with Peter Brook I began to take care, once I had got a performance to a certain point, to keep it exactly the same—allowing always, of course, for certain gradations over many performances. There obviously has to be a certain amount of flexibility, but now I am sure it is most important to keep the main lines the same. For many years I had been far too much inclined to make experiments in a part, especially in a long run, and also, of course, in plays which I had also directed myself, so that I was accountable to

231

no-one but myself in making changes. Occasionally I would alter things for the better, but it is better discipline to simplify rather than to elaborate.

If you want to earn your living in the theatre you are bound to be in some failures during your career. All the great people — Edith Evans, Laurence Olivier, Peggy Ashcroft — have had their failures at one time or another. It is very interesting, looking back, to see why certain things went wrong. When Beaumont was alive I used sometimes to stay with him at weekends to try to discuss some production in which he was concerned which had failed, but his other friends would say 'Not to be mentioned in this house. It's dynamite.' It seems to me that when a play is a failure it is fascinating, once the disappointment has worn off, to examine where you went wrong. A play is always a great experiment. The director, the cast, the way that rehearsals proceed, the rows with the designer, the different ways the play goes during a try-out — all these things contribute. It is very important, when it is all over, to look back and see where the mistakes were, because you work just as hard in a failure as in a success.

It is also possible to achieve personal success in a failed play. Laurence Olivier made his name in three plays that failed with the critics and the public — *Beau Geste*, *The Circle of Chalk* with Anna May Wong, and *The Rats of Norway* by Keith Winter. In all three plays he got superb notices personally, so that in a curious way it made his career to be in failures — a comforting thought for young actors!

I am inclined to be rather too impressed by adverse notices and less impressed by good ones. If I am praised too much I think the critics are overdoing it and I cannot be as good as they say. If I am savagely attacked, I think I cannot be quite as bad as all that. But I am inclined to think that one learns more from bad notices than from good ones. If a critic praises a certain detail in your performance it is apt to make you very self-conscious. You go on the next night thinking 'This is the bit they say I do so well' — and find you cannot do it any more. Notices ought to be constructive and I do not like it when they are personal. I was very shocked when two of our important critics criticized a recent play and mentioned by name other actors who, they considered, would have been more suitable for the parts than the actors who played them. I think that is inexcusable, as are remarks about an actor's physical appearance. I could never quite forgive James Agate, who was rather a friend of mine and helped me very much in my early career, for what he said about Dorothy Green. Dorothy, who was then about forty-five and was in *Antony and Cleopatra* with me at the Old Vic, and very effective in the part, had an extremely large nose. In his notice of the production Agate said 'Miss Green, like a battleship, commands from the bridge' which I thought was cheap and hurtful.

Nor do I like the idea that critics should be invited to watch rehearsals. I think that would be the greatest possible mistake. Too much is known nowadays, both by the critics and the public, about the quarrels of actors and the intimate difficulties of production. In the old days these things were private, closely kept secrets which you did not discuss even among your fellow actors. You should not bite the hand that feeds you and you should not be disloyal to or spiteful about people you may not like. You cannot go through your life without making enemies (and friends too, thank God) but it is difficult to strike exactly the right balance and not to hurt people's feelings at some time or another in the theatre.

Some of our best players hate to feel that they are being showy. The natural dignity and reserve of English people (even of actors) makes them ashamed to think that they may be showing off. Ralph Richardson, for instance, is very aware of this. Edith Evans was never happy even taking a call at the end of a play. She did so only because it was polite and customary. Leon Quartermaine, with whom I played for many years, was an exquisite and delicate actor, and he, too, always seemed to resent the show-off part of the theatre—the advertisements, the gossip, the publicity, the interviews and so on. I have tried to follow their example, though I must admit I do not feel I have always succeeded. If you do not quite receive the respect and appreciation which you know you have earned, it is rather galling and can make you bitter. I am always surprised one does not meet more embittered actors.

I am quite useless at almost everything except where the theatre is concerned and so I have always been completely occupied working there. It has never bothered me that I do not like all the things that occupy most people in their spare time. I am rather solitary in some ways and I prefer to be, though I have had wonderful friendships and associations in the theatre all my life—with painters, designers, musicians and actors—and travelled an enormous amount. What more can one ask?

I am not good at being idle. I have had a few memorable holidays and, of course, in making films one always has a great many days off; but as I have no family I do not have the urge to take holidays that most people have. I feel useless if I have not got a job and I have been very lucky in being asked to appear in films or on television or make records if I have had no play in mind. Although I live much more inside the walls of a theatre than anywhere else, I still love being out of doors in the country or watching and meeting people in cities. But I have had my share of parties and large gatherings—and no longer crave the excitement I used to feel at being successful. Acting has rid me of my frustrations and satisfied many of my ambitions. It is more than an occupation or a profession; for me it has been a life.

Biographical Notes

by John Miller

CHAPTER ONE: *1904–1921*

1. **Kate Terry** was the first of the Terrys to make their name famous on the English stage. At the age of eight she had been engaged by Mr and Mrs Charles Kean, the very successful actor-managers, to play in pantomime, then to play Prince Arthur in *King John*, and at the age of fourteen her Cordelia brought her immediate stardom. She acted with the then unknown Henry Irving in Manchester, played Ophelia to Fechter's Hamlet in London, but gave up her brilliant stage career when she married Arthur Lewis. She did not return until thirty-one years later, playing a small part in support of her daughter, Mabel Terry-Lewis, with John Hare in *The Master*.

2. **Ellen Terry** followed her elder sister Kate into Mr and Mrs Charles Kean's company. After her debut in their production of *The Winter's Tale*, she was also a notable Puck, Prince Arthur and Fleance in *Macbeth*. At sixteen she met her first husband, the forty-seven-year-old artist G. F. Watts, when he was painting Kate. The marriage was short-lived, and probably never consummated. Later she created a scandal by running away to live with Edward Godwin, leaving the stage for six years. Henry Irving asked her to become his leading lady in 1878, beginning with her playing Ophelia to his Hamlet. During their partnership of twenty-four years, she gave memorable performances of Portia, Beatrice, Desdemona, Viola, Lady Macbeth, Cordelia, Imogen and Volumnia, as well as supporting Irving in many of the melodramas for which he was famous, some of them specially written for him.

    Ellen's long partnership with Irving is thought now to have been more than just professional, though no breath of scandal touched either of them at the time. She had two other short-lived marriages to rather unsuccessful actors—Charles Kelly in 1878 and James Carew in 1906, when she was fifty-eight and he was thirty-two.

    In 1903 she made a near-catastrophic experiment in management, with her son Gordon Craig directing her in Ibsen's *The Vikings*, which only ran for twenty-four performances. In 1906 she finally succumbed to Bernard Shaw's pleas to play the part he had written for her—Lady Cecily Waynflete in *Captain Brassbound's Conversion*. After 1906 her stage appearances were infrequent, but her lecture tours of America and Australia were very popular. John Gielgud saw her lecture on 'Shakespeare's Heroines', and in later years he approached his own *Ages of Man* recital in much the same way, sketching in just an impression of

235

some characters, and acting full-out only in the long set-piece speeches. She was created a Dame in 1925.

3. **Henry Irving** acted with five members of the Terry family—Kate, Ellen, Marion, Florence and Fred—but it is his long partnership with Ellen that is best remembered. His strange diction and rather awkward gait were handicaps in his youth, and he was thirty-three before he achieved overnight fame as the haunted murderer Mathias in *The Bells.* He revived it many times, and Ellen Terry said it was the emotional strain of this part that finally killed him. For three decades he dominated the stage as a tragedian of great power and intensity and a comedian of grim sardonic humour. He was rewarded with the first knighthood ever conferred on an actor in 1895.

4. **Edith and Gordon Craig.** Ellen Terry chose the name Craig for her two illegitimate children while on a Scottish holiday, after a great rock off the coast of Ayrshire—Ailsa Craig. Edith travelled abroad as her mother's stage-manager and finally took up directing but without much success. Gordon Craig also acted with his mother and Henry Irving, but after directing her disastrously in *The Vikings* he spent most of his life in different parts of Europe, drawing, designing, occasionally directing and writing prolifically. He founded and edited *The Mask,* a journal on the art of the theatre, and ran a school of acting in Florence. His books had a great effect on methods of production in Europe and America.

5. **Marion Terry** first appeared on stage in 1873, as Ophelia in Tom Taylor's corrupt version of *Hamlet.* She stepped into her sister's role as Viola in *Twelfth Night* when Ellen was suffering from a poisoned thumb in 1884, and substituted for her on several other occasions. She played for the Bancrofts, Beerbohm Tree, with Henry Irving in *Faust,* in several seasons with George Alexander and with Charles Wyndham. Her greatest successes were in light comedy, especially in Wilde. Even though she never achieved Ellen Terry's stature, she toured England and America, and was rarely out of work in a career that spanned fifty years.

   She was an enthusiastic supporter of John Gielgud and wrote to her brother Fred about Gielgud's 1930 Hamlet at the Old Vic, 'It's *very young,* very thoughtful (without dragging it with long pauses and mouthing), graceful without effort and every word distinct and of course he looks charming—I told him I was proud of my nephew, he replied he "was proud of knowing he had some of the Terry blood in him, and hoped to go on doing better".'

6. **Fred Terry** was the youngest child in the family that gave three famous leading ladies to the English stage and would have given a fourth, had Florence not retired on her marriage. He first appeared at the age of sixteen in the Bancrofts' revival of *Money,* and then played with his sister Ellen in *New Men and Old Acres.* He played Sebastian to her Viola in Irving's disastrous production of *Twelfth Night.* Irving's Malvolio was booed, Ellen collapsed from a horse-fly bite and was replaced by Marion, and only Fred's performance received unanimous praise. In 1900 he went into management with *Sweet Nell of Old Drury,* playing King Charles to his wife Julia Neilson's Nell Gwynne. This was revived many

times over the next twenty years. He also played Benedick in *Much Ado About Nothing* with great success.

7. **Frank Benson** made his first major appearance on the stage as Clytemnestra in Aeschylus' *Agamemnon* in the original Greek, at Oxford, produced by him in 1880 and then taken to London, where it greatly impressed Ellen Terry and Henry Irving. His first professional appearance was as Paris to their *Romeo and Juliet* in 1882. In 1883 he went into management and began the tours, mostly of Shakespeare's plays, for which he became famous. Many of the productions came to London for short seasons and a regular fixture was the week-long annual Stratford Festival, where he laid the foundations for a season in Shakespeare's birthplace that now runs for most of the year. At one time he had as many as four touring companies on the road, and they became widely recognized as training grounds for all serious actors. He was the only actor to have been knighted in a theatre (still wearing his blood-stained toga from his performance as Caesar).

8. **Herbert Beerbohm Tree** went into management for himself in 1887, and was generally accepted as the successor to Henry Irving in the line of actor-managers. He built Her Majesty's Theatre, and managed it from 1897 until he died in 1917. It was here that he staged his famous Shakespeare Festivals with huge casts, spectacular scenery and effects, and often real animals on the stage (rabbits in *A Midsummer Night's Dream,* and his King Richard II entering London on horseback). His casual approach to the intentions of playwrights led to a series of battles with Bernard Shaw, whose play, *Pygmalion,* he was the first to produce in 1914. Virtually every leading Shakespearian player of the time appeared with Tree. In 1904 he founded the Academy of Dramatic Art (later RADA), and was knighted in 1909. He died in 1917.

    Gerald du Maurier excelled in playing English gentlemen. He was very successful in Barrie's *The Admirable Crichton* and *Peter Pan,* in which he created the parts of Captain Hook and Mr. Darling. He was also a highly successful actor-manager, nearly always producing modern or recent plays. He was knighted in 1922.

9. **Charles Hawtrey,** born in 1858, was a successful actor-manager who performed in many comedies and farces. He was known for his gentlemanly liars, spendthrifts and erring husbands. As a skilled teacher of acting, had a profound influence on Noël Coward. He was knighted in 1922 and died in 1923.

10. **Mabel Terry-Lewis** made her theatrical debut in 1895, aged twenty-three. She retired and returned to the theatre after an absence of fifteen years. She built a very successful career for herself after her new start at forty-eight. She first appeared in New York in 1923, and in 1930 played Lady Bracknell in Wilde's *The Importance of Being Earnest,* with her nephew John Gielgud as John Worthing.

11. **Squire Bancroft** (1841–1926), together with his wife Marie, successfully managed the Prince of Wales Theatre and later the Haymarket. They

presented and played in many drawing-room comedies, and helped to put the acting profession on a securer footing by giving good salaries and paying for costumes.

Johnston Forbes-Robertson, born in 1853, was an even more successful actor-manager. He appeared with the Bancrofts and with Irving. He took over the management of the Lyceum in 1895 and his Hamlet there was much admired, particularly for the beauty of his voice and the grace of his movements. In the tradition of great acting families, he had three brothers and a nephew also on the stage. He was knighted in 1913, the year of his retirement, and lived to be eighty-five.

12. **Eleonora Duse** was born in 1858 into an Italian acting family—the Duse troupe founded by her grandfather Luigi. Her first success came in Verona, as Juliet, at fourteen, one of the rare occasions when an actress has succeeded in the part at the correct age. After seeing Sarah Bernhardt in Turin, she appeared in several of Dumas' plays, and her fame began to rival that of her French contemporary, especially in *La Dame aux Camélias*. She was a naturalistic actress who refused to wear make-up, and was famous for being able to pale or blush at will.

Unconventional and unhappy in her private life, she was a charming comedienne, but excelled in the great tragic parts, and at the end of her career triumphed as Clytemnestra, Antigone, Electra, and as several of Ibsen's heroines. Of her 1923 tour St John Ervine wrote: 'She has the power which no other actress, known to me, possesses, of transmitting physical qualities to her very clothes; when she drops her shawl from her shoulders at the end of the second act after a period of trouble, it seems to be as weary as she is, to have gathered weariness into its folds, so that it drops almost to the ground in sheer fatigue.' This tour continued in the United States to packed houses, but she caught pneumonia in Pittsburgh and died on 21 April 1924. She was given a funeral mass in New York, and a state funeral in Rome.

13. **Sarah Bernhardt** became the most talked-about actress of her day after appearing as Racine's Phèdre at the Comédie Française. She was known for her eccentric private life and displays of temperament. She took up painting, sculpture and ballooning and, after the early death of her sister Régina, was said to keep her own satin-lined coffin in her bedroom and sometimes to sleep in it. When she arrived in England in 1879 with the Comédie Française she was met by Oscar Wilde, who christened her 'The Divine Sarah.' She formed her own company and toured America, where she triumphed as Camille in Dumas' play. In Paris she had successes in plays by Dumas, Sardou and Rostand and in the title-roles of Hamlet and Lorenzaccio, which opened the Théâtre Sarah Bernhardt. She drew huge crowds on her frequent world tours. Slim and striking to look at, her greatest attribute was her 'golden voice.' The French critic Françisque Sarcey described it as 'languishing and tender, her delivery so true in rhythm and so clear in utterance that never a syllable is lost, even when the words float from her lips like a caress.' After a stage accident, she had to have a leg amputated at the age of seventy, but continued to appear in recitals, sketches and an occasional play, even

though she was carried to the stage. She died in 1923 at the age of seventy-eight.

14. **Madge Kendal** was the twenty-second child of an actor-manager, and sister of the dramatist T. W. Robinson, but is best known for her long partnership with her husband William Kendal, and John Hare at the St James's Theatre. She was a fine comedienne and is most remembered for her performances in contemporary plays. The companies with which she and her husband were connected, until her retirement in 1908, were an important training-ground for young actors and actresses, and their partnership was held up as a model for the profession. She died in 1935.

15. **Oscar Asche** was born in Australia in 1871 and sent by his Norwegian father to Norway to learn acting. Later, in England, he joined Benson's Company, then Sir Herbert Tree's. He partnered Ellen Terry in her disastrous venture into management, but later under his own management won great success with such lavish spectacles as *Kismet* and other extravagant productions of musicals and Shakespeare. He wrote the lyrics and dialogue of *Chu-Chin-Chow,* to music by Frederick Norton, and produced and starred in it with his wife Lily Brayton. It ran for five years in London, beginning in 1916.

16. **Harley Granville-Barker** was one of the most influential theatrical figures of the early years of this century. Born in 1877, he went on stage at the age of fourteen. He worked with Tree and with William Poel, and in 1900 Shaw chose him for the part of Marchbanks in *Candida.* He played in and produced many of Shaw's plays, and several of his own. In *Man and Superman* he played John Tanner opposite Lillah McCarthy, who became his first wife. He wrote *Waste, The Marrying of Ann Leete, The Voysey Inheritance, The Madras House, Rococo* and a number of adaptations. His productions of Shakespeare just before the First World War broke away from Tree's expensive spectacular style and revolutionized the whole approach to text.

   In 1914 he went to America, fell in love with Helen Huntingdon and divorced his first wife to marry her in 1918. She persuaded him to devote himself to writing and lecturing, a decision that his old friend and collaborator Bernard Shaw denounced as a public scandal at one of Granville-Barker's own lectures. His most important publications were his five volumes of *Prefaces to Shakespeare,* published between 1927 and 1947. He exerted a profound influence on John Gielgud when they worked together on *Hamlet* and *Lear.*

CHAPTER TWO: *1922–1928*

1. **Claude Rains** first appeared on the London stage as a child actor in *Sweet Nell of Old Drury* in 1900, then performed with Granville-Barker in his 1914 tour of the USA. After the First World War he made a name as a character actor as well as a leading man. In 1926 he went to America to tour in *The Constant Nymph* and spent a number of seasons with the Theatre Guild in New York. He made his film debut in 1933 as *The*

Invisible Man, in which his face was bandaged entirely. For the next sixteen years he worked in films, including *Anthony Adverse, The Adventures of Robin Hood, Mr. Smith Goes to Washington, Casablanca, The Phantom of the Opera* and *Caesar and Cleopatra.* He died in 1967.

2. **Sybil Thorndike** went to the Old Vic in 1914, and returned many times to play virtually all the great Shakespeare female roles and also such male parts as Prince Hal in *Henry IV,* the Fool in *King Lear,* and Puck in *A Midsummer Night's Dream.* She had great successes as Hecuba in *The Trojan Women* and as Medea. In 1924 she created the role of *Saint Joan,* and went on to play many of Shaw's heroines—he once described her as his ideal Candida. She performed in many contemporary plays—*A Day by the Sea* with John Gielgud, *Separate Tables, The Potting Shed, The Chalk Garden.* She often acted with, or was directed by, her husband Lewis Casson, and in later years they gave dramatic or poetry recitals together all over the world. She was created a Dame in 1931. She continued acting until arthritis forced her to retire from the stage in 1969. She died in 1976 at the age of ninety-four.

3. **Lewis Casson,** an influential actor and director, co-directed, with Bernard Shaw, the 1924 production of *Saint Joan,* in which he performed with his wife Sybil Thorndike. He acted with Olivier and Ralph Richardson with the Old Vic, with Helen Hayes on Broadway in *Victoria Regina,* and directed Gielgud in *Lear* in 1940 with Granville-Barker. He was knighted in 1945 and died in 1969 at the age of ninety-three.

4. **George Devine,** born in 1910, was President of the Oxford University Dramatic Society (OUDS) when he invited John Gielgud to produce *Romeo and Juliet* in 1931. He acted with Gielgud many times, including in his 1935 *Hamlet,* and co-directed and acted in his 1955 *Lear* in London and on tour. As an actor-manager, he discovered and encouraged such new-wave dramatists as John Osborne. He died in 1966.

5. **Nigel Playfair** first acted with the OUDS, then toured with Benson's Company, appeared in several of Shaw's plays, in Shakespeare with Tree, and played Bottom in Granville-Barker's famous production of *A Midsummer Night's Dream* in 1912. He ran the Lyric Theatre, Hammersmith, from 1918 to 1932, and was knighted in 1928. He died in 1934.

6. **Noel Coward** was very successful as a child actor. He became a good friend of John Gielgud, who succeeded him in *The Vortex* in 1925, and again the following year as Lewis Dodd in Margaret Kennedy's *The Constant Nymph.* In 1956 Gielgud starred in his play *Nude with Violin.* A prolific songwriter and playwright, his most successful plays were *Hay Fever, Bitter Sweet, Private Lives, Cavalcade, Design for Living, Tonight at 8:30, Blithe Spirit* and *Present Laughter.*

7. **Gwen Ffrangcon-Davies** was a well-established actress by the time she played Juliet to John Gielgud's first Romeo. They appeared together many times in the 1920's and 1930's. She played his wife in the wartime *Macbeth,* his daughter Regan in the 1950 *Lear,* and his mother in Gra-

ham Greene's *The Potting Shed* in 1958. He directed her in *The Cherry Orchard* with Trevor Howard, and brought her into the American tour of his production of *The School for Scandal.*

8. **Barry Jackson** founded England's first theatre especially designed for a repertory company in Birmingham in 1913. In London he directed many productions of Shaw and introduced Pirandello, Margaret Leighton, Paul Scofield and Peter Brook to the public. In 1946, he became Director of the Shakespeare Festival at Stratford-on-Avon. He was knighted in 1925 and died in 1961.

9. **Mrs Patrick Campbell** first appeared on stage at Liverpool in 1888. She caught the public's attention in *The Second Mrs. Tanqueray* with George Alexander in 1893. Bernard Shaw wrote *Pygmalion* for her, and she created the part of Eliza Doolittle at the age of fifty, and revived it several times. She performed in several of Ibsen's plays, including as Hedda Gabler and as John Gielgud's mother in *Ghosts.* In her youth she was outstandingly beautiful, and her talent and her devastating wit made her one of the great theatrical figures of her time. She carried on a long correspondence, and possibly a love-affair, with Bernard Shaw; their letters were published after her death in 1940 and formed the basis of the play *Dear Liar.*

10. **James Agate,** born in 1877, was the most influential drama critic of his day. He wrote for the *Saturday Review,* then for the *Sunday Times,* and was also drama critic for the BBC. He died in 1947.

11. **Edith Evans** was discovered by William Poel, who offered her first a small part in his revival of a sixth-century Hindu classic *Sakuntala* and then the lead opposite Esmé Percy in *Troilus and Cressida,* both in 1912. She was twenty-five but quickly made up for her late start. She toured with Ellen Terry, appeared in Sir Barry Jackson's production of Shaw's *Back to Methuselah* in 1923, and joined the Old Vic in 1925. Her appearances with Gielgud include Juliet's nurse, Lady Bracknell, Katerina in *Crime and Punishment,* and Katharine of Aragon in *Henry VIII.* He has also directed her in *The Old Ladies* and *The Chalk Garden.* She had many great successes in modern plays, but the playwrights with whom she will be most associated are Shakespeare, Congreve, Wilde and Chekhov. She partnered Redgrave, Richardson and Olivier, but her most scintillating performances were with Gielgud. She was created a Dame in 1946 and died in 1976.

CHAPTER THREE: *1929–1930*

1. **Harcourt Williams** made his first appearance on stage with Benson in *Henry V* in Belfast in 1898. He toured with Ellen Terry, Henry Irving and George Alexander and was seen in new plays by Ibsen, Shaw and Granville-Barker. In 1929 he was appointed producer at the Old Vic and persuaded John Gielgud to join the company, which attracted a wider public

to its performances. He continued to act and produce until near the end of his life in 1957.

2. **Lilian Baylis,** born in 1874, interrupted a musical career in South Africa in 1895 to return to England and help her aunt run a temperance hall, the old Victoria Theatre—to become the Old Vic. After her aunt's death in 1912, she turned the theatre into a place where opera and drama could be brought to ordinary people. All Shakespeare's plays were produced there between 1917 and 1923. She opened the Sadler's Wells in 1931 for opera and ballet and it was equally successful.

3. **Hamlet** is the part most associated with the first half of John Gielgud's career. His first performance of it in 1929 was an instant success. James Agate wrote: 'This actor is young, thoughtful, clever, sensitive; his performance is subtle, brilliant, vigorous, imaginative, tender and full of the right kind of ironic humour. . . . It is the high water mark of English Shakespearian acting in our time.' Sybil Thorndike wrote to him: 'When you spoke your final word I said to myself what I said when I read the first chapter of *Moby Dick:* "This is too good to be true".'

  In 1934 Gielgud directed himself in the part for the first time and worked on the designs with the Motleys. The cast included Jessica Tandy as Ophelia and the young Alec Guinness in his very first part, as Osric. It ran for 155 performances, a record beaten until then only by Henry Irving.

  In the 1936 production in America, he played Hamlet with Judith Anderson as the Queen and Lillian Gish as Ophelia. He played and directed *Hamlet* again in 1939 at Kronborg Castle, Elsinore, and for a week in London. George Rylands directed him when he played the part for the last time in 1944, with Peggy Ashcroft as Ophelia and Leslie Banks as the King. Agate thought this was his best Hamlet: 'Mr Gielgud is now completely and authoritatively master of this tremendous part. . . . He has acquired an almost Irvingesque quality of pathos, and in the passages after the play scene an incisiveness, a raillery, a mordancy worthy of the Old Man. He imposes on us this play's questing feverishness. . . . In short, I hold that this is, and is likely to remain, the best Hamlet of our time.'

4. **Leslie Howard,** the son of Hungarian immigrants, came to epitomize the shy English gentleman, especially in his Hollywood career. After he was discharged from the Army in 1917 suffering from shell-shock, he quickly established himself as a leading man on the stage in London and New York, where he scored a great success with Tallulah Bankhead in *Her Cardboard Lover.* In the thirties he acted principally in America in films, with Bette Davis in *Of Human Bondage,* with Humphrey Bogart in *The Petrified Forest,* with Vivien Leigh and Clark Gable in *Gone With the Wind,* and with Ingrid Bergman in *Intermezzo.* His Shakespearian roles were much less successful—his Broadway Hamlet suffered by comparison with John Gielgud's and the 1936 MGM film of *Romeo and Juliet,* in which he was Romeo to Norma Shearer's Juliet, was one of the most disastrous Shakespeare films to come out of Hollywood. When the Second World War broke out he returned to England and made a number of patriotic films as actor-director. He was killed in 1943 when his plane was shot

down in a flight from Lisbon to London, in rather mysterious circumstances.

5. **Richard Burton,** born in 1925 in Wales, performed with the OUDS while attending Oxford. He was discovered by Emlyn Williams, who gave him his first professional part in *Druid's Rest. The Lady's Not for Burning,* his earliest appearance with John Gielgud, ran for a year in London and opened on Broadway in 1950. His first Hamlet, in 1953 at the Old Vic, was compared to Gielgud's debut twenty-four years before. He has performed on Broadway with Helen Hayes in *Time Remembered* in 1957, with Julie Andrews in *Camelot* in 1960, and in Gielgud's 1964 *Hamlet,* the most profitable Shakespeare stage production ever. His film appearances include *Look Back in Anger, Cleopatra, The Spy Who Came in from the Cold* and *Who's Afraid of Virginia Woolf?*

6. **Ralph Richardson** performed with a touring company for four years before joining Barry Jackson at the Birmingham Rep in 1925. He joined the Old Vic in 1930, and his first part was Prince Hal in *Henry IV Part I,* with John Gielgud as Hotspur. They have played together in many productions and their different styles have complemented each other so well that they have enjoyed a remarkable joint success. Considered among the first Shakespearian actors on the English stage, Richardson has said: 'An actor tackling classical roles is like a jockey on a famous horse which many great jockeys have ridden, there's a 25 per cent chance you won't get it over the jumps. But as a professional you are used to being afraid. You accept fear.'

   With Olivier he led the revived Old Vic company from 1944 to 1947, appearing as Peer Gynt, Falstaff and Cyrano de Bergerac. His notable associations with John Gielgud have been in the latter's production of *The School for Scandal* in London in 1962, *Home* in London and in New York in 1970 and *No Man's Land* in London and in New York in 1975.

CHAPTER FOUR: *1931–1938*

1. **Theodore Komisarjevsky** was born in Venice in 1882, brought up in Russia and in the pre-Revolutionary theatre there. His sister was the famous Russian actress Vera Komisarjevskaya, and he did his first production at her theatre in St Petersburg in 1907. He was later made director of the Imperial and State Theatres in Moscow. In 1919 he came to England to produce Borodin's *Prince Igor* at Covent Garden. He was also a very skilled designer, and his season of Russian plays at the tiny Barnes Theatre (in 1924–25) in which John Gielgud performed attracted notice.

   His later Shakespeare productions at Stratford-on-Avon aroused controversy: a *Macbeth* with aluminum scenery and modern uniforms, and *The Merry Wives of Windsor* with a Viennese background and fairies with lighted candles on their heads. In 1936, he went to live in America.

2. **Michel St-Denis** was the nephew of the great French director Jacques Copeau, and began his career with him at the Vieux-Colombier as stage-

manager and assistant producer. In 1931 St-Denis took over the direction of his uncle's company, reorganizing it as the Compagnie des Quinze. Although the company lasted only three years, it established a considerable international reputation. In 1935 he came to England and produced *Noah,* in which John Gielgud acted, and in 1938 he also directed the fa-mous *Three Sisters* with Gielgud, Peggy Ashcroft, Michael Redgrave, Alec Guinness and Gwen Ffrangcon-Davies, when John Gielgud was in management with his own company. The two of them worked together in *The Cherry Orchard* in 1961, with Peggy Ashcroft. A sensitive and imaginative director, he was deeply interested in the training of actors. He ran the London Theatre Studio from 1936 to 1939; after the Second World War he was head of the Old Vic School, and when it closed he returned to France to direct the Centre Dramatique de l'Est in Strasbourg. In addition he was artistic adviser to the Lincoln Center Project in New York, and to the Royal Shakespeare Theatre.

3. **Peggy Ashcroft** has been directed by John Gielgud, or performed opposite him, since 1932, when she and Edith Evans played Juliet and the Nurse in his production of *Romeo and Juliet* for the OUDS. She has played Ophelia to his Hamlet, Cordelia to his Lear, Emilia to his 1961 Othello and, most memorably, Beatrice to his Benedick. Her performances in Ibsen, Chekhov, Henry James's *The Heiress,* Beckett's *Happy Days,* Enid Bagnold's *Chalk Garden* and Rattigan's *The Deep Blue Sea* attracted both critical and public acclaim. Created a Dame in 1956, she has also been honoured by having the Ashcroft Theatre at Croydon named after her in 1962.

4. **Marie Tempest** starred in comic opera between 1885 and 1899, and then abandoned her singing career to become the leading comedienne of the next four decades. She had great success in the title role in *The Marriage of Kitty,* which she played many times in London and on a world tour that lasted five years, and as Judith Bliss in the first production of *Hay Fever,* and Olivia in *Mr Pim Passes By.* Gielgud played with her in *Dear Octopus* in 1939. She was created a Dame in 1937, and continued acting until she died in 1942 at the age of seventy-eight.

5. **Violet Vanbrugh** was the elder of the Vanbrugh sisters. She toured America with the Kendals, played with Irving in 1891, and understudied Ellen Terry as Cordelia in *Lear* and Rosamund in *Becket.* She was most successful playing a series of society ladies.

Irene Vanbrugh was five years younger than Violet, and was more successful. She played with most of the great actor-managers over the years. She became recognised as an outstanding interpreter of the plays of Barrie and Pinero, and had successes in plays by Wilde and Maugham. She was created a Dame in 1941.

6. **Madge Titheradge** was born in Melbourne in 1887 and first appeared on the London stage in *The Water Babies* in 1902. She performed in the title-role in *Peter Pan,* Fisher in *The Admirable Crichton,* and included in her classical parts Desdemona, Beatrice, and Nora in *A Doll's House.* She specialized in playing grand titled ladies. She died in 1961.

7. **Lillah McCarthy,** the first wife of Harley Granville-Barker, created the leading roles in many Shaw plays, including *Man and Superman, The Doctor's Dilemma* and *Androcles and the Lion.* She went into management in 1911, playing Hilda Wangel in Ibsen's *The Master Builder,* and playing Shakespearian roles with her husband.

8. **Ruth Draper,** born in America in 1884, toured in dramatic monologues written by herself. She won great acclaim for her ability to act the roles of several different people at the same time or to respond to invisible characters.

CHAPTER FIVE: *1939–1945*

1. **Baroness Blixen** was born Karen Dinesen in Denmark in 1885. She studied English at Oxford University and painting in Paris and Rome. In 1914 she married her cousin, Baron Blixen, and went with him to run a coffee plantation in British East Africa. When they were divorced, in 1921, she took over the management of the farm herself and 'began to write . . . to amuse myself in the rainy season'. She returned to Europe in 1931 and in 1934 she published *Seven Gothic Tales* under the name of Isak Dinesen. Among her later works are *Out of Africa,* published in 1937, and *Winter's Tales,* published in 1942. She died in September 1962.

2. **Hugh 'Binkie' Beaumont,** born in 1908, was probably the most successful impresario of the twentieth-century British theatre. He was notable for matching plays with the best possible actors, directors and designers, and was famous for his association with John Gielgud. Among the shows he put on were *Dear Octopus, The Heiress, The Lady's Not For Burning, A Day by the Sea, Nude with Violin* and *The Potting Shed,* which starred or were directed by Gielgud. His successful musicals were *Oklahoma!, Irma La Douce, West Side Story, Hello Dolly!* and *My Fair Lady.* He died in 1973.

CHAPTER SIX: *1946–1954*

1. **Esmé Percy** acted with Granville-Barker in 1908, and then with Annie Horniman, the great promoter of repertory theatre, in Manchester. An authority on Shaw, in 1949 he became president of the Shaw Society.

2. **Peter Brook,** born in 1925, has often aroused controversy with the experimental methods he has used in his productions, especially of Shakespeare, since 1946. He directed Paul Scofield as Hamlet in 1955, and as Lear in a famous production for the Royal Shakespeare Company in 1962 which toured abroad to great acclaim and was later filmed. More recent productions include Weiss's *Marat/Sade, US,* a documentary on the American presence in Vietnam, and the influential *A Midsummer Night's Dream* for the RSC, which used trapezes, jugglers and other circus techniques.

    In recent years he has taken companies to Iran and Africa and experimented with new forms of drama, using legend, myth and contemporary documentary techniques woven together with music and mime. His experimental studio is based in Paris.

3. During the run of *Venice Preserv'd,* John Gielgud's knighthood was announced. His first line in the play was 'My Lord, I am not that abject wretch you think me,' which stopped the play the night of the announcement with an ovation of cheering and applause that carried on for several minutes.

CHAPTER SEVEN: *1955–1978*

1. **Alain Resnais** decided to make *Providence,* his first English-dialogue film, as soon as he saw David Mercer's script, although Eric Shorter speculated in *The Daily Telegraph* that 'perhaps English is not the right language for the expression in the cinema of high-flown sentiments and low-tone comedy which shows an actor of Gielgud's quality in situations of Wildean irony and uninhibited agony.' In 1977 the film won most of the French cinema awards, for best French film of the year, best direction, script, sound, editing, music and design, and shortly afterwards the New York film critics voted Gielgud the Best Actor of the Year for his performance as Clive Langham.

2. **Orson Welles** shot *Chimes at Midnight* very quickly, but he had conceived it over many years. In his early days with the Mercury Theatre in New York he once combined eight of Shakespeare's history plays into a cut-up version of his own called *Five Kings.* In 1960 he put *Chimes at Midnight* on the stage in Belfast. It draws together a selection of the Falstaff scenes from both parts of *Henry IV* and *The Merry Wives of Windsor,* plus dialogue from *Richard II, Henry V* and Holinshed's Chronicles. Welles described it as a lament for the death of Merrie England. He made it into a film in 1966 and only had Gielgud for two weeks to shoot his scenes as the King, a part that was nearly as long as Falstaff's in the film. He shot no retakes, and used doubles for Falstaff's own scenes. In spite of all these constraints, it is generally considered one of Welles' finest films, with particularly moving performances by Gielgud, Welles, and Keith Baxter as Prince Hal.

CHAPTER EIGHT: *America*

1. **Irene Worth** was born in America and made her debut on Broadway in 1943 in *The Two Mrs. Carrolls.* She went to England for her theatrical training and remained there for most of her career, returning to the USA to live only in recent years. She has appeared in classic roles with the Old Vic and the Royal Shakespeare Company and has gained her greatest recognition for her tragic parts. In 1953 she worked with John Gielgud for the first time, in his production of *A Day by the Sea.* They later peformed together in *The Potting Shed, The Ides of March* and *Oedipus* in London; *Tiny Alice* in the United States (for which she won a Tony award); and toured North and South America in *Men and Women of Shakespeare.*

246

2. **Helen Hayes,** who was born in 1900, made her first Broadway appearance at the age of five as Prince Charles in *The Royal Family*. In 1927 she starred in Jed Harris's production of *Coquette* in New York and then on tour, and married the playwright Charles MacArthur. Her most famous role was as the English Queen in *Victoria Regina*, which ran from December 1935 until January 1939, breaking box-office records in New York and on its tour of forty-three United States cities. Her first performance in London was as Amanda Wingfield in John Gielgud's production of *The Glass Menagerie*. In 1955 she received the honour of having a Broadway theatre named after her.

3. **The Lunts** formed their famous partnership when they married in 1922. Lynn Fontanne was born and brought up in England, where she had acting lessons with Ellen Terry, but her first success was in America. Alfred Lunt was an American from the Midwest who made his name on tour. They performed together in Noël Coward's *Design for Living*, but it was their performances in *The Taming of the Shrew*, *Idiot's Delight*, *Amphitryon 38* and *The Seagull* that established them as unquestionably the most famous acting team in America and London. Renowned for their comic playing, their unique trick of overlapping their lines and their torrid lovemaking on stage, the Lunts have been compared, as partners, to Henry Irving and Ellen Terry. Their long career together ended with Alfred's death in 1977.

Hamlet, from *Stage* magazine, June 1937. A caricature by A. Birnbaum

Index

Italic figures indicate black and white illustrations. Pl. indicates the numbered colour plates

249